W9-AMZ-635

The KOD System.

Current stage of development

Johann Vielberth

in collaboration with the research associates
of the eufo-institute

Regensburg 2008

Institute for Development and Research Dr. Vielberth regd. Co.

ISBN 978-3-9812532-1-4

Vielberth Johann et al: The KOD System. Current stage of
development. Regensburg 2008, Institute for Development and
Research Dr. Vielberth regd. Co.

With the collaboration of

Abbas Amin ▫ **Andrea Ewels** ▫ **Shan Guan** ▫ **Larissa Li** ▫ **Craig Mabrey** ▫ **Eva Mittermaier** ▫ **Sabine Plum**

Table of Contents:

1. Preface

KOD is the name of an international communication system. It is designed as an auxiliary tool that facilitates international communication, offering the possibility to cope with the diversity of languages.

The completed system will have a fundamental impact on all possibilities of international communication: It enables people to understand the content and structure of texts in foreign languages which are represented in KOD. The use of KOD furthermore empowers speakers of any language to participate in international exchange on equal footing.

The present document describes the construction of the system, shows possible forms of its application and exemplifies the long-term potential it contains.

The KOD system is based on a concept of Dr. Vielberth's. An international linguistic research group has been concentrating on the realization of this concept in coordination with Dr. Vielberth at the "Institut für Entwicklung und Forschung Dr. Vielberth e.K." (hereafter "eufo-institute") in Regensburg since 2000.

An initial description of the basic idea and of the primary research fields of the KOD project was presented in 2006[1].

The system has been further developed since that time. It is now possible to show the connection and the interaction of its various components more clearly than was possible in 2006. In particular the

---

[1] Vielberth, Johann: The KOD Communication System, Reflections on the idea, realization and prospects of a new tool for international communication. This volume is available at the eufo-institute in Regensburg.

functionality and efficiency of the system can be very precisely demonstrated on the basis of transparent examples.

At the same time the general pre-conditions for the development of the system have changed somewhat. In the meantime a multitude of translation programmes and translation support tools for many languages are available on the software market and in the internet. For this reason it is important

- to reveal KOD's logical relationship to the predominant approaches to such translation supported by automatic language processing,
- to determine the advantages it provides and
- to demonstrate the way in which it can be expediently integrated into such approaches.

With this new report a current description of the KOD project will be added to the project description of 2006 in order to document the internal progress of the project and the modified state of affairs.

The present volume was written to be understood on its own. It is therefore unavoidable that some contents of the last volume will be repeated especially where basic aspects of the concept of KOD are concerned.

All in all the thematic focus of the project has shifted noticeably compared to its early stage. The present report will take this into account by concentrating on the current focal areas.

Conclusive project research described in detail in the first KOD report with no alterations in the course of further development will only be briefly outlined to include essential results as far as necessary for complete comprehension.

A detailed summary of the surveys done in the fields of phonetics, graphemic construction and international words is appended to this volume.

The essence of language is human activity – activity on the part of one individual to make himself understood by another, and activity on the part of that other to understand what was on the mind of the first. These two individuals, the producer and the recipient of language [...] should never be lost sight of if we want to understand the nature of language [...] (Jespersen 1924/1992: 17)

2. KOD as a communication system

2.1. The basic idea: a uniform representation scheme for all languages of the world

The basic idea of the KOD system is to provide a standardized notation suitable to depict potentially all natural languages. It is exactly this idea which motivates the name of the system: "KOD" (an abbreviation for "coding") stands first for the process of depicting a language by means of the KOD system and secondly for the inventory of depiction elements, which are the main components of the system.

Speakers of all languages should be able to participate actively in international communication using their respective native language and its cultural context as a starting point and then articulating themselves using KOD. The representation of each language takes place in KOD true to its original structure – as far as possible. No rules or differentiations should be imposed on the speaker of a language, which are unknown in his own language. Such a point of departure insures that speakers of all languages have equal and likewise easy access to international communication via KOD. The KOD procedure is in accordance with the principal that everybody starts from his own language.

The standardized depiction makes similarities and equivalences[2] visible which exist among the languages integrated in KOD. For the recipient of a message who has mastered the system this uniform representation offers a basis for the comprehension of the encoded text.

To the extent that certain grammatical functions and regularities in an encoded language are unknown to the recipient, he or she will need additional explanations which the system then provides in the form of instructions which enable the recipient to decide upon the proper interpretation (interpretation assistance).

The KOD system does not provide its own grammar in the form of standardized word-order or a binding inventory of labels for grammatical functions. It is restricted to the reproduction of the morpho-syntactical identification elements existing in a language and leaves the word-order rules of the language to be encoded unchanged.

2.2. Means for language depiction in KOD

The basic structure of the communication process made possible by the system is, therefore, outlined in simplified form as follows.

---

[2] Normally only partial equivalences exist between the expressions of different languages. Roman Jakobson (1959) therefore characterizes the relation between the terms of individual languages as "equivalence in difference". Jakobson, Roman (1959): On Linguistic Aspects of Translation. In: Brower, R.A. (ed.) On Translation, Cambridge, MA, Harvard University Press, p. 234

Participants are

- the encoder: the person who encodes texts or expressions of his mother tongue or his preferred language
- the means which are provided by the system for this purpose
- the recipient: a person who can comprehend the encoded texts using his knowledge of the system.

The described relationships can be seen in the following diagram:

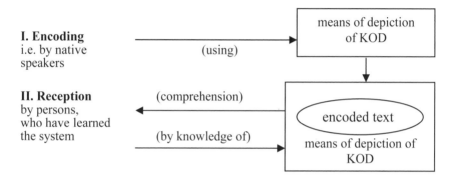

Diagram 1: Encoding and comprehension of encoded texts

The KOD system comprises two basic types of depiction:

- KOD-markers, that are strings of characters which serve for the representation of grammatical functions, and
- KOD-lexemes, that are strings of characters which represent word contents.

Words of different languages are not depicted in their potentially ambiguous range of use in the system. KOD-lexemes rather refer to unique meanings of these words and are – other than words in natural languages – unambiguous.[3]

The strings of literal characters, which serve as a means of depiction within KOD, were created artificially.[4] In doing so both types of depiction were intentionally differentiated, so that they can be easily identified.

KOD-markers are composed as *vowel-consonant-vowel*. For example *afe, ani, eba*.

KOD-lexemes constitute the phonetic counterpart to markers. They are composed as *consonant-vowel-consonant*. In order to construct larger words these basic elements can if need be extended by the addition of a further *vowel-consonant* unit. For example *nug, nugam, nugatim*.

Within the KOD-system markers and lexemes are the reference point for two processes - as described above: they serve, on the one hand, to either encode or render languages and constitute, on the other hand, the basis of the comprehension process that KOD enables.

The inventory of forms of depiction used for encoding a language in KOD is admittedly only a subset of the total inventory which KOD provides for the representation of all languages and is essential for the receptive comprehension of encoded texts. Accordingly it is necessary to differentiate the respective components of the system.

---

[3] Connotations, which are each bound to specific terms of individual languages and with their historical development cannot, however, be considered when mapped into KOD.

[4] The considerations applied in the formation of such literal strings are explained extensively in chapter 3.4, cf. also appendix I.

2.3. Components of the KOD system

A component named KOD-global is essential for the receptive comprehension of texts. According to the basic idea of the system KOD-global comprises those lexemes and markers which depict contents of words and grammatical functions in any language insofar as two conditions are fulfilled:

- They must exist in a plurality of languages, meaning that they do not represent a unique characteristic of one specific language.[5]
- They must be part of the basic or advanced learner's vocabulary and should therefore be frequently used.

These two criteria: (a) interlinguistic distribution and (b) the noticeably frequent use[6] of lexical meanings and grammatical functions in various languages define the range favouring the development of standardized forms which are meaningful for rendition and therefore significant for international communication.

The sum of lexemes and markers which constitutes KOD-global is composed of those forms of depictions that have been developed

---

[5] The existence of grammatical functions or a lexical meaning in at least two languages is only one of several criteria identifying the relevance of a given linguistic form for KOD. Additionally considerations were taken into account which concerned factors like volume and the geographical range of the language concerned as well as the significance of the country within the global communication process.

[6] Data about word use frequency differ according to type of text, topic and communication sector. The established frequency of a word available in corpora alone is not a sufficient criterion for the delimitation of the relevant field of vocabulary. Therefore different procedures are combined at the eufo-institute (orientation to the basic vocabulary lists and dictionaries; estimations of learning theory for foreign languages) in order to approach the desired categorization heuristically.

for a great number of typologically different languages.[7] KOD-global is not a closed set, however, it reaches such a high degree of coverage that only slight modifications or extensions will become necessary when new languages are integrated into the system.

KOD-global is supplemented by a component including those words and possible grammatical functions for every integrated language which are often used in that particular language but not to be found in other languages: KOD-special. For each language adapted to KOD such a special component exists.

The grammatical categories integrated in KOD-special are associated with an already established category label and their grammatical functions appropriately described. Words belonging to the KOD-special component retain their original form as far as possible and are furnished with an explanation, which is to be retrievable in any of all the languages integrated in the system. In the case that the specific writing system of the respective language is not the Roman alphabet, KOD-special includes transliteration conventions. These conventions determine how words and grammatical forms are rendered in languages for which KOD-global provides no direct means of depiction. With the aid of these transcription guidelines not only words of the KOD-special-component can be depicted but also words beyond the domain of the vocabulary defined as KOD-global.

---

[7] In particular the following languages were involved in the development of the system: Arabic, Bulgarian, Chinese, Croatian, English, Finnish, German, Greek, Hindi, Hungarian, Italian, Japanese, Russian, Spanish, Turkish, and Yorùbá. Moreover, in the development of the system research results from applied and comparative philology over and beyond the scope of these languages were taken into account.

KOD-global	KOD-
Grammatical functions and basic word contents which occur in more than one language	special

Diagram 2: main components of the system: KOD-global and KOD-special

For elements of vocabulary which have neither been incorporated in KOD-global nor in KOD-special interfaces to available dictionary resources are foreseen.

With the aid of these dictionaries a user can independently construct a supplementary vocabulary module which can be extended according to the requirements of the system.

For the rendition of a single language in KOD only a specific selection from the KOD-global-inventory is used. In this respect a distinction must be made between the KOD-lingual component of a language and the larger inventory of KOD-global. The KOD-lingual component of a language encompasses part of the KOD-global depiction system and a sub-set of KOD-special.

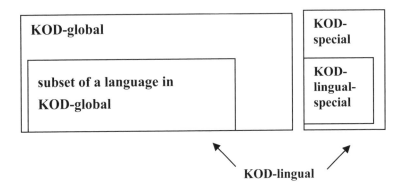

Diagram 3: The relation between KOD-global and KOD-lingual

The part of the total inventory of KOD-global used as the KOD-lingual component of a language does not constitute a fixed range but differs from one language to another. Furthermore, the actual formal implementation of meanings and the respective grammatical functions is different depending on the language. One and the same grammatical function may be expressed differently depending on the language considered. Such a function may be expressed by an irregular word form in one language while another language uses a suffix (a word-ending), an auxiliary or a function word. For that reason it is also necessary to concretely confirm how each language can best render those KOD-global depiction forms.

In order to understand more sophisticated texts of a given language the recipient who masters KOD-global must also familiarize himself with the KOD-lingual-special components of that language. The fraction of KOD-lingual-special does differ from language to language. However, it remains small and will therefore not demand much additional study.

2.4. *Operative interaction of the components*

Using the described system texts of any source language can be encoded, that means converted into KOD. When encoding the native speaker takes recourse to the KOD-global-units appropriate for his own language and if need be also to those extensions offered by the KOD-lingual-special component. Thus he produces an accurate structural mapping of the current text. Less frequently used words for which KOD provides no lexemes may be included in their original form without any explanation in the encoded text. The recipient must look up the meaning of these words in normal dictionaries if necessary.

The following diagram demonstrates the interaction procedure.

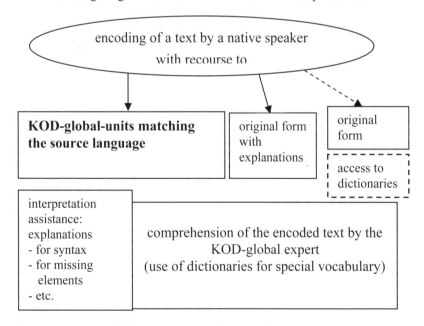

Diagram 4: use of KOD-components when encoding

The KOD recipient is offered a representation of the underlying text or expression via KOD. In doing so he is expected to cope - to a certain extent - with the structures, which he does not know in his own language: he encounters phrases encoded from other languages, for example, with other grammatical functions or words which are strung together in another sequence than in his own language. Information may possibly be missing which he needs in order to form correct phrases in his own language. In order to facilitate the treatment of such discrepancies and to train intuition the system provides information about differences which exist between certain language pairs or between language types. Thus the system offers support to users making quick and clear understanding of the source texts possible despite such differences.

Basically the KOD system relies intentionally on the human capacity to quickly learn the management of different structural patterns and to flexibly respond to them.

2.5. Computer assistance when using KOD

Despite maintaining the principle that the computer assistance is not fundamentally necessary, enhancements based on automatic procedures of language processing are conceivable. This would minimize the effort of the human user and the possible sources of error when encoding and thereby increase the efficiency of the system.

One possibility to realize this goal could, for example, be a preliminary analysis – based on the specific characterization of the languages chosen to be converted into KOD.

By using established methods of automatic speech analysis the encoding process could be considerably simplified. Conceivable additions would be the process of automatic segmentation, speech recognition and syntactic analysis. The manual encoding process could thereby be reduced to the case where an automatic analysis failed or its implementation would entail disproportionally high effort. This concerns, for instance, many ambiguities existing in one language. They must be differentiated to determine which of the many possible meanings of a word in a given text is meant.

After a text has been encoded it would be possible to automatically make adjustments to simplify the reception of the encoded text for the speaker of a given language. Generally such adjustment procedures must refer to a pair of particular languages or language types. Differences in the word order of a language could be realigned this way or syntactical constructions could be replaced which do not exist in the target language.

The following diagram demonstrates the way the up- and downstream mechanisms of language processing (shaded in the chart) can be integrated in the use of KOD.

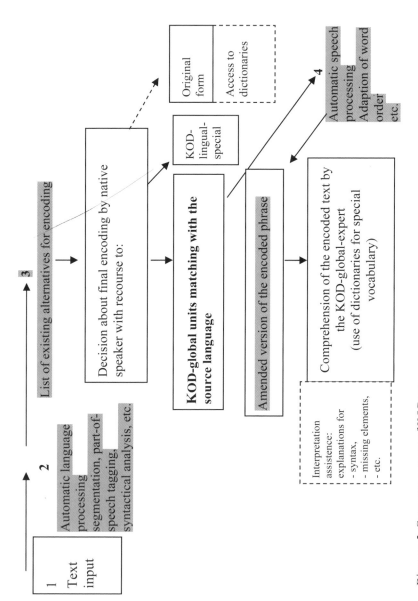

Diagram 5: Computer support of KOD use

24

By using appropriate procedures for the conversion of encoded phrases into an individual language the form in which these texts are presented could be construed to be more similar to the surface structural conventions familiar to the addressee in that language. For comprehension of the exported text less language specific knowledge and thereby less training effort would be necessary. A great deal of the otherwise necessary interpretation aids and explanations might prove superfluous for this reason.

2.6. Structure of this volume

The current description of the structure and use of KOD has revealed that KOD-global is the pivotal aspect for the operation of the system. The KOD-global inventory provides the means for consistent representation of grammatical functions and word contents and thereby decisively guarantees interlinguistic comprehension, which is the aim of KOD.

The detailed description of the development and the current state of this inventory therefore constitutes the beginning of an elaborated presentation (corroborated by examples) found in the next chapter. (chapter 3)

The development of such an inventory is a challenge in many respects: on the one hand concise limits for the necessary degree of coverage, which such an inventory should have, are difficult to define, especially in the field of vocabulary. On the other hand difficulties must be overcome which are fundamentally implied by the comparison of typologically distant languages.

The procedures applied in the development and some examples of the results achieved will be described in more detail in the immediately following chapter. In this case distinctions are made between the research in the fields of grammar and vocabulary, which led to the definition of the content of the KOD-markers and KOD-lexemes, and that research dealing with the phonetic and graphemic composition of markers and lexemes.

The following chapter (chapter 4) focuses on the integration of different languages in the KOD system. It explains the consequences resulting from the elaboration of the KOD-lingual components in detail.

The two following chapters (chapter 5 and 6) deal more intensively with the two processes which need to be taken into consideration in conjunction with the use of the KOD system. They contain examples of different languages and are particularly easy to follow without any special theoretical knowledge. First, the process of encoding is placed in the spotlight (chapter 5). The subsequent chapter is devoted to reception, the comprehension of encoded texts. (chapter 6)

Additional options for the use of the system and for conceivable application scenarios will be discussed in the ensuing chapter. (chapter 7)

The possibility of computer support using KOD is analyzed in the penultimate chapter of this volume (chapter 8) where the focus bears on the relationship between KOD and approaches to automatic translation and on the possible status of KOD as a component of a partially automatic language transmission operation.

3. Development of KOD-global

3.1. General framework

In 2000 Dr. Johann Vielberth collected a team of linguists of different nationalities and launched the KOD project at the Institut für Entwicklung und Forschung Dr. Vielberth e.K. in Regensburg. The institute and the project are financed solely by him. Its goal was the gradual implementation of Dr. Vielberth's concept for the KOD system.

The development of KOD-global, which will be described in the following, constituted the main focus of the project in the first years (2001-2006). KOD-global was to be developed as a comprehensive inventory of notational media which include all grammatical categories occurring frequently in the language of the world. In order to guarantee that KOD-global achieves a high degree of coverage the following languages were involved in the development:

Arabic, Bulgarian, Chinese, Croatian, English, Finnish, German, Greek, Hindi, Hungarian, Italian, Japanese, Russian, Spanish, Turkish and Yorùbá.

The basis for selecting these languages were criteria such as the total number of native speakers, membership in certain language families and global economic status.[8]

---

[8] Chinese, for example, (including second language speakers) is by all counts the number one language in the world with approximately one billion speakers. It is followed by English with 350 million native speakers (whereby the role of English as the official administrative language in many countries as well as the large number of second language speakers is not taken into consideration). There are more than 200 million estimated native

On the one hand these languages formed the basis for the development of KOD-global by the Regensburg research team, which analyzed them as representatives of different language families. On the other hand the results of applied and comparative linguistics as well as fundamental surveys concerning linguistic universals and typological approaches were also consulted and incorporated.

3.2. Construction of KOD-markers with respect to content

As mentioned above KOD-markers are systematic notational elements representing grammatical functions. According to the basic idea of the system markers are to be placed in an encoded text at the position where the presence of a certain grammatical function is indicated by morphological signals (inflectional endings or mutation in a paradigm) or where a corresponding function is expressed by so-called function words (independent morphemes). Accordingly the placement of a KOD-marker would presuppose the presence of physical evidence or, in the linguistic sense the "marking" of a grammatical form in the source language.[9]

Encoding would then iconically preserve the structural integrity of the source language.

---

speakers of Hindi, Russian and Spanish, respectively, just under 200 million speakers of Arabic, more than 100 million of both German and Japanese. Italian ranges just above 50 million speakers and Yorùbá just below. For further reference cf. Campbell, G.L. 2000. Compendium of the World's Languages (2nd edition) London: Routledge

[9] Accordingly only the parts of an opposition pair which are formally distinguished can be considered as marked. For example 'grammatical number' realised as singular and 'grammatical tense' realised as present are not overtly marked in most languages in contrast to the overt marking they may assume for other values, i.e. plural or past tense.

When implementing this approach certain constraints had to be respected. On the one hand a system had to be developed which not only takes the idea of a mapping for a single language into consideration but which also adequately illuminates the relationship existing between different languages. This means that the initial differentiation between existence and absence of a grammatical category in a certain language must be considered. The starting point for introducing a KOD-marker must be the existence of a grammatical opposition in a language, not the physical presence or non-presence of a certain category value.

For instance, Chinese verbs do not have a tense category. English and German verbs do, although present tense is generally not overtly indicated. Nevertheless the opposition (present tense – past tense) is valid. Chinese will, therefore, use a non-marked form. English and German, in contrast, must always use a tense marker when encoding a finite verb form.

On the other hand irregular forms and syncretism[10] in languages limit the possibility to comply with the above principles for preserving their structural integrity in an unrestricted sense.

In addition, the aspect of structural iconicity mentioned above is not, however, the main objective of the KOD system.[11] It is rather

---

[10] C.f. Bickel, Balthasar /Nichols, Johanna (2007) *Inflectional Morphology*, in: Shopen, Timothy (ed) (2007) *Language typology and syntactic description.* vol. 3 p. 207f; Baerman, Matthew/Brown, Dunstan (2005a) and (2005b) in: Haspelmath, Martin et al (2005) (eds.) p. 118-125.
[11] In this sense KOD is fundamentally different from the process of grammatical glossing which tries to represent all grammatical categories of a definite language as accurately as possible with respect to linguistic standards. cf. The Leipzig Glossing Rules: Conventions for interlinear

more important that the KOD-markers take on the challenge of adequately explaining the functional content of those grammatical categories existing in a language. In doing so, knowledge about the respective grammatical category and the allocation of the corresponding KOD-markers should be transparent for the native speaker without needing special linguistic training. For this reason a great deal of weight was placed on the content of the KOD-markers during the development of KOD-global.

3.2.1. Inventory of grammatical categories

As a starting point for the development of KOD-global grammatical functions were compiled yielding a comprehensive inventory of all the morpho-syntactic forms of the languages examined and describing their respective functions in detail. As far as the languages in question permitted, the parts-of-speech of traditional Latin grammar were utilized. Initially they served as sorting and cataloguing criteria to structure the large amount of grammatical information involved. In a first step, a classification of categories was established, which is morphologically associated with those words belonging to different word categories or parts-of-speech in the various languages (i.e. "case" and "number" for nouns). At the same time the values associated with these categories in the different languages were collected e.g. 'singular', 'dual' or 'plural' as instances of the category "number".

---

morpheme-by-morpheme glosses. A revised version can be consulted at http://www.eva.mpg.de/lingua/pdf/LGR08.02.05.pdf or http://www.eva.mpg.de/lingua/resources/glossing-rules.php 2008.

The classification of parts-of-speech is, however, not standardized for all the languages of the world. In addition, semantic, morphological and syntactic categories can play varying roles in the traditional differentiation of parts-of-speech, so that a clear cut distinction between the different terms used for parts-of-speech is not possible. Assigning words of structurally very different languages to word classes whose definition have their roots in the "authoritative" tradition of Latin grammar has often been very justly criticized. In a second step the resulting categories were therefore uncoupled from the traditional 'Latin' differentiation for parts-of-speech, in order to encompass all the languages in which the categorization of parts-of-speech is controversial or at least does not follow the traditional differentiation.[12]

The inventoried data was subjected to a comparative analysis. For each category examined, functional values were collected to determine which elements were present in a plurality of languages or were only represented in a single language of those analyzed at the eufo-institute. These results subsequently served as the starting point for an examination based on current research in the areas of typology and comparative linguistics.

In some areas, however, it proved quite difficult to analytically evaluate the data. Both the terminology and the functional explanations applied to the respective categories were inconsistent. In many cases the terms used actually confused existing functional similarities rather than clarifying them.

---

[12] This is, for example, the case in Chinese where words can only be identified as belonging to a certain part-of-speech through their function in a sentence.

In order to solve the problems discovered a collection of differentiation functions was compiled based on existing research in comparative linguistics, thereby identifying those functional elements essential for such categorizations. The advantage of this approach lie in the use of standardized description patterns. These patterns effectively permitted the alignment of classification categories occurring in different languages.

3.2.2. Differentiation functions as the basis for a compilation

With the functional descriptions thus compiled an initial platform was reached from which the correlation of grammatical categories in typologically different languages became possible.

Within the context of their functions in different languages the formally differently implemented patterns may be considered analogous. For example synthetic forms of one language correspond to analytical forms in another language. In German the future tense is analytical (*ich werde gehen*), in Italian it is synthetic (*andrò*). Along the same lines, the comparative in German (*schöner*) is synthetic, but equivalent to the analytical comparative in Italian (*più bello*), while the comparative in English can be implemented either synthetically (*faster*) or analytically (*more beautiful*) depending on the length of the adjective.

There are other instances where functional conformance between inflectional categories and lexical elements is visible. From a functional point of view prepositional phrases are often comparable with morphological case endings and likewise constructions with modal verbs correspond to functions of the grammatical category mood. Similarly, in certain languages, constructions with serial verbs fulfil functions, which are expressed in other languages by the grammatical categories of mood and tense.

In this tenor, when judging whether these functions are analogous or even constitute partial equivalents in different languages, only the main "prototypical" grammatical function of these categories can be considered decisive. This applies in particular when comparing languages which are very distant to each other.

In general grammatical forms have different functions. However, descriptive grammars usually only identify the main function of the category concerned.[13] Therefore, a further specific linguistic examination must take place to determine to which extent derivative functions of the examined forms found in texts are sufficiently covered by the established inventory. This is accomplished by the incorporation of concrete text examples when integrating single languages into the KOD system.

This is also the case with respect to the degree of differentiation used when encoding. It is necessary to verify the applicability of the established inventory.

When identifying categories linked to functions it proved to be difficult to distinguish between the lexical meaning - which a form as such furnishes in a text - and the selective restrictions of meanings only provided in certain concrete contexts. Grammatical description surveys do not always respect this differentiation[14]. When in the

---

[13] Cf. Bickel, Balthasar/Nichols, Johanna (2007). Inflectional Morphology. In Shopen, Timothy (ed.) *Language typology and syntactic description.* vol. 3, p. 211 as applied to case descriptions

[14] Bernard Comrie describes the relevance of this differentiation and the difficulties connected with it in several of his works. Cf. Comrie, Bernard (1998) Ein Strukturrahmen für deskriptive Grammatiken. Allgemeine

context of the language instruction, for example, a complete listing of all existing uses of a category would be preferred, the tendency is an exhaustive list, which however, does not reflect the linguistic classification of such different uses.

Among other considerations this methodical approach is in great danger of a failing to adequately represent the semantic-functional unity of a category due to the one-sided concentration on the function of the grammatical category by favouring an excessively detailed description of its function.

The question, for example, whether or not the German tense category 'present' can be mapped to several functions defined by different representation conventions can only be answered definitively, when the interaction of different languages related to a significant number of contexts has been analyzed.

3.2.3. Established grammatical functions

The initial results of the described inventory and analysis were around 300[15] functional components, i. e. grammatical concepts, which emerged as the values existing within categorizations of particular categories in the languages examined.

Within the scope of further development modifications in this inventory became necessary. They are based on further analyses

---

Bemerkungen. In Zaefferer (1998) p. 9 as well as Comrie (1985/2000) p. 23-26.

[15] A table of the grammatical categories analyzed and of the number of markers developed for their rendition is found in the volume 'The KOD Communication System – Reflections on the idea, realization and prospects of a new tool for international communication, 2006'. This table lists 294 basic KOD-markers and 27 spare forms for not yet completely justified functional concepts derived from a review of typological linguistic research.

which were performed at the eufo-institute in the last few years. In this connection the compiled functions were assigned to grammatical forms of different languages for test purposes. (cf. also 4.1.) On the basis of these allocations texts and phrases were subsequently encoded where these forms appeared. During these tests grammatical functions were uncovered in some places which had not yet been fully taken into consideration; such additions were, however, normally only necessary to cover secondary functions of an existing grammatical form.

Moreover, these tests revealed differences between languages which must be better born in mind when implementing KOD. This observation led to the refinement of the already compiled function templates for KOD.

Currently the total inventory of the identified grammatical functions assigned to the different grammatical categories can be summarized as follows:

Grammatical categories	Number
person (1., 2., 3. person; general)	4
number (singular, plural, dual)	3
semantic categories (+/- human, +/- animated, gender)	6
tense (present, past, future; anterior, posterior; proximal and distal)	10
aspect (i. e. perfective, imperfective, continuous, iterative, habitual, etc.)	9
voice (active, static passive, in general passive)	3
mood (i. e. necessary, probable, factual, non-factual, etc.)	38
gradation (comparative, superlative, elative)	7
definiteness/indefiniteness	3

semantic case functions (i. e. temporal, local, modal, etc.)	155
negation	1
emphasis	2
courtesy	2
syntactic functions	9
Placeholders (for semantically empty elements)	5
pronouns (basic forms) (personal, possessive and relative pronouns)	38
conjunctions, connectors	54
classifiers	1
interrogative pronouns	11
deixis	9
total	366

Table 1: Inventory of KOD-markers

The different values for the functions of conjunctions or connectors were not differentiated in the diagram of 2006.

In as far as the examination of the compiled inventory could not be conducted in all categories, it can be expected that modifications and minor adjustments will crop up in the inventory during further development. Where particular areas of grammar are concerned, for instance the range of grammatical mood which is subject to significant fluctuations concerning the functions of grammatical categories, most classical grammatical reference books offer no reliable orientation.

3.3. Treatment of vocabulary

The semantic contents of the frequently used words of the general vocabulary are to be expressed by unique KOD-lexemes in KOD. The definitions for these semantic contents had to be distilled through the examination of basic vocabularies for the languages analyzed at the eufo-institute.

The actual process of forging vocabulary was done based on thematically defined vocabulary ranges, thus facilitating a more precise assessment of the complexity and efficiency of the vocabulary concerned. In addition such a process simplifies the control of expedient guidelines, for instance to guarantee systematic integrity when defining meanings in particular areas of vocabulary.

3.3.1. Thematic groups

Apart from the 'function words' which are considered a part of the field of grammar, the important basic areas of vocabulary can be summarized under specific topics as follows:

- numbers
- colours
- weekdays
- names of months
- elementary temporal and locational adverbs
- names of seasons
- sensory qualities
- words for body parts
- kinship relations
- professions

- social behaviour
- body activity in general
- intellectual activity
- sports
- animals
- plants
- clothing
- dwellings

In fact, for thematic groups defined in this way the associated words cannot generally be explicitly delimited or allocated. Nevertheless such keywords do indeed offer enough orientation to compile and describe the respective central word concepts as a point of departure for further vocabulary development.

The advantage of this approach lies in the reorganization into small and concise groups of the generally confusingly number of potential concepts resulting from research and comparative examination for different languages. Phenomena which occur in specific lexical areas thus become more accessible and more easily subjected to consistent treatment.

Large sections of the vocabulary cannot be approached and classified in this way. Therefore additional exemplary texts topicalizing everyday life were also consulted to expand the vocabulary.

The vocabulary goal set for KOD-global encompasses around 35,000 lexemes each of which represent a single content, a meaning. This quantity is anticipated to yield a high degree of coverage for common everyday text types occurring in different languages. Approximately one third of this total volume has been compiled.

3.3.2. Special areas of the vocabulary: routine phrases, idiomatic expressions

Aside from words that have a specific meaning and regularly occur as such in changing sentence contexts, all natural languages possess a stock of idiomatic expressions, figures of speech and routine phrases, which can only be understood adequately as complete entities. For this reason, conventional or idiomatic phrases are treated separately in dictionaries of different languages. They can frequently be found as a supplement in the final part of dictionary articles about a lemma.

Within certain language families there are partial correlations between the metaphoric imagery of expressions and the literal meaning of empty figures of speech. However, taking culturally and typologically distant languages into consideration the differences to be found in different languages become far more significant. Thus the imagery and pragmatic functions of language expressions are frequently impossible to derive from the literal meaning of the individual words used.

The verbatim word-for-word transmission of such figures of speech into the KOD system bears the potential danger that the user of the system will not understand them. However, it is even more dangerous that they may evoke misunderstandings, yielding un-noticed false conceptual anchors for the comprehension of the suc-cessive contents, especially for longer texts. This must be avoided by all means.

Therefore, specific phrases, idiomatic phrases and routine formu-las constitute a special area of the KOD vocabulary. Inasmuch as they can be represented by elements of KOD-global, they are encoded according to special guidelines. For the range of routine formulas a system for representation was developed by which both the formulistic character and the pragmatic function of the respective formula in a language can be distinguished. Thus misunderstandings are avoided which occur by an interpretation, which takes the lexemes used in the formula too literally. (cf. for example "How do you do?" as a question of emotional status in English in contrast to the functionally corresponding Finnish formula "Mitä kuuluu?", which literally means "Heard anything?".)

Similarly idiomatic phrases are marked indicating that they have a specific meaning as a unit, which deviates from the literal meaning of their parts.

3.3.3. International words and proper names

Within the KOD system there are two further areas requiring special treatment, namely international words and proper names.

Due to their wide distribution within many languages international words are often seen as that part of vocabulary which facilitates international communication as well as the acquisition of a foreign language. In fact international words can only partially fulfil this task because they are not necessarily known in all languages to a comparable degree and furthermore only apply to certain areas of the lexicon. Nevertheless international words which have reached widespread distribution in different languages have been intentionally integrated in the KOD lexicon.[16]

---

[16] An investigation about the distribution of the selected international words was carried out for the languages represented at the eufo-institute. Cf. Appendix III

When defining the literal strings used to represent internationally widespread words in KOD it was fundamentally important to guarantee their recognition as international words. This is the reason why international words in KOD deviate partially from the phonetic-graphemic and phonotactical rules which otherwise identify KOD-lexemes. International words exhibit, for example, diphthongs, consonant clusters und double vowels, which are otherwise not permitted in KOD-global, cf. *autobiografia, administrasion, ballet, bestseller*, etc.

Proper names are characterized by the fact that they help identify the named person or the labelled object. This is not normally completely achieved by the meaning of the word or words used as a name[17]; very often such word meanings have been lost or have faded over time provided that they ever existed.

As a result the phonetic-graphical composition of literal strings used in names is much more important than in other parts of the vocabulary.[18] For this reason KOD permits, in principal, the use of the original forms of different languages when forming names. Languages, which do not use the Roman alphabet, must additionally represent these names in accordance with the transcription rules valid for their language.

The Roman alphabet is also used to transcribe some important proper names which constitute a part of KOD-global. They are internationally known names for countries, places and institutions,

---

[17] Different naming conventions exist in different languages. This also applies to the importance placed on the meaning of the literal string used as a name.

[18] Legal regulation makes reference to this with respect to copyright and trademark conventions.

etc. and have their own individual name in different languages. Where geographic phenomena of a specific country are concerned, the conventional name used in this country yields the standard form in KOD. In this point KOD concurs with the efforts of the UN to standardize geographic names.[19]

---

[19] Cf. UNGEGN publicity brochure, retrievable at:
http://unstats.un.org/unsd/geoinfo/toponymyguidelines.htm

3.4. Phonetics

3.4.1. Phonetic inventory and phonotactics

One focal point of the development of KOD lies in the compilation, systematization and definition of comparable grammatical functions and word contents across languages as described above. All research dealing with the phonetic and graphemic definition of KOD elements encompassed a large field of research in itself.

Basic phonemes were identified based on comparative linguistic analyses. The results led to the formation of literal strings for KOD elements. Criteria for the selection of the phonetic segments and their systematic mapping to phonemes were, on the one hand, the widespread appearance of corresponding phonetic segments in the world languages and, on the other hand, the frequency with which such differentiated phonetic characteristics were considered phonemic.[20]

Characters of the Latin alphabet were allocated to the resulting 25 phonemes[21] – as follows:

---

[20] With respect to selection and mapping cf. Appendix I

[21] In the volume 'The KOD Communication System – Reflections on the idea, realization and prospects of a new tool for international communication, 2006', the diphthongs <ai> and <au> were listed as elements of the phoneme inventory of KOD, which contained 27 phonemes including these. Because the use of diphthongs affects the segmentation and thereby also the semantic transparency of KOD-markers and KOD-lexemes it was subsequently decided not to include them in the phoneme inventory of KOD.

	KOD-phoneme	spelling
1	/a/	\<a>
2	/b/	\<b>
3	/d/	\<d>
4	/e/	\<e>
5	/f/	\<f>
6	/g/	\<g>
7	/h/	\<h>
8	/i/	\<i>
9	/j/	\<y>
10	/k/	\<k>
11	/m/	\<m>
12	/n/	\<n>
13	/ŋ/	\<ng>
14	/o/	\<o>
15	/p/	\<p>
16	/r/ [22]	\<r>
17	/s/	\<s>
18	/ʃ/	\<sh>
19	/t/	\<t>
20	/tʃ/	\<ch>
21	/u/	\<u>
22	/x/	\<x>
23	/v/ [23]	\<w>
24	/z/	\<z>
25	/ʒ/	\<j>

Table 2: KOD-phonemes and graphemes

Evidence from foreign language teaching indicates that syllable structures with consonant clusters at the morphological boundaries are prone to increased learning difficulties for speakers of certain

---

[22] pronunciation variants [r], [ʀ], [ʁ], [l] cf. Appendix I

[23] pronunciation variants [w], [v]

languages.[24] This resulted in the decision to give preference to a simply constructed syllable structure for KOD and to avoid clustering of consonants as much as possible.

The further consequential decision to differentiate between alternate syllabic forms for KOD-markers and KOD-lexemes permits a clear distinction between both of these types of representation within the KOD system.

3.4.2. Simple and bundled markers, marker combinations

For each function determined a specific marker was composed according to the formation principles described above.

Primary tests showed, however, that the results of using these markers produced unacceptably long chains of word elements and that when further developing KOD-markers it must be taken into consideration to which proportion the identified grammatical categories occur in the languages investigated. In fusional inflecting languages grammatical marking can represent more than one grammatical category at the same time being condensed, e. g. the verb ending in German, in which person, number and tense together constitute a single unit.

In order to take this factor into account and to permit shorter word forms in KOD, in addition to the markers which stand for a single grammatical function, further markers were composed which can subsume two to three grammatical functions in the triple-character phonetic form of the type vCv (vowel-consonant-vowel). In doing so each single phoneme signifies specific grammatical information so

---

[24] cf. Maas, Utz (1999): Phonologie. Opladen/Wiesbaden: Westdeutscher Verlag, p. 237.

that comparable word forms of a specific language can be represented with significantly shorter and more economical combinations than would be possible using single markers.

The first position of the following markers is mapped, for instance, to the category "number" (a = singular, e = plural), the second position to the category "tense" (n = present tense, t = past tense, etc.) and the third position to the category "person" (a = 1st person, i = 2nd person, e = 3rd person): *ana, ani, ane* (1st, 2nd, 3rd person, singular, present tense); *ata, ati, ate* (the corresponding forms for the past tense) as well as *ena, eni, ene* and *eta, eti, ete* for plural forms.

Beside the markers for the above mentioned single functions 123 markers in total were developed, which bundle several grammatical functions according to the principles described above. These bundled markers do not represent further grammatical functions but rather represent another form of rendition for information already covered by other single KOD-markers. The internal logic in the formation of these combined KOD-markers guarantees ease of acquisition, as well.

Bundled markers must be differentiated from marker combinations where several single markers are strung together to render the meaning of a certain element in a language. For example, the bundled marker *aza* (inflected definite article in German) corresponds to the marker combination *ivi* (=definite) *-ova* (=singular) - *ora* (=nominative).[25]

---

[25] The phonetic structure of some markers is still only preliminary, because changes can arise as a consequence of systematic considerations.

3.4.3. Creation of KOD-lexemes and the treatment of word composition

Formation patterns exist in all languages with which existing vocabulary can be expanded and be adapted to the needs for new expressions. Comparative studies on word formation and the respective derivation patterns, which were carried out at the eufo-institute, revealed that some of these construction patterns are widespread within the languages of the world.

However, when comparing specific areas of the vocabulary with regard to formation structures very often the differences are what prevail. It must be concluded that not necessarily the formation patterns themselves are incompatible but that their application is often to a great extent subject to linguistic restrictions found in specific individual languages.

The phonological realization of elements defined for the established contents through the formation process of KOD-lexemes is, for this reason, not oriented to the structure which the underlying words of the different languages have. The basis for the use of specific derivation procedures is rather located in the defined meanings developed for respective KOD-lexemes.[26]

The use of such procedures should contribute to the ease with which certain areas of the vocabulary of KOD can be understood due to the systematic regularities embedded in them.

---

[26] Thus the logical connection between the word „steal", [to illegally take away property] and the word "thief", [somebody who illegally takes away property of another person] is made visible by the fact that the KOD-lexeme for "thief" (*kerefos*) derives from the verb "to steal" (*keref*). Notice however that the representation form in KOD is valid independent of the form, in which corresponding contents are expressed in different languages.

Furthermore certain word formation elements were defined with which the vocabulary volume of KOD can be extended at any time. Such word formation elements are either constructed as a combination of "consonant + vowel" (Cv), so that they can be prefixed to an already existing KOD-lexeme or they are formed as "vowel+consonant" (vC) and can be used as a compositional suffix.

A further possibility for the extended use of the KOD vocabulary is established by specific serialization principles for word composition[27] in specific languages using already existing words.

On the basis of his knowledge of the KOD system the recipient can in such cases at least understand the parts of individual constructions. To what extent he is able to adequately understand the total meaning of the composition depends in many cases on the respective context.

---

[27] The specific order of 'specifiers' and 'heads' for a given language is to be explained in a catalogue of accompanying interpretation guidelines.

4. Development of the KOD-lingual components

The inventory of the KOD-markers and a portion of the KOD-vocabulary were initially developed in independent research modules as a sub-section of KOD-global.

Up to the year 2006 comparative tests and analyses of existing grammatical descriptions for different languages formed the basis for the development of the marker inventory.

In order to verify and to further refine the compiled inventory in connection with the concrete use of finished parts of the vocabulary, the eufo-institute elaborated the KOD-lingual components for Arabic, Chinese, English, German, Hungarian, Italian and Russian in the years 2006 and 2007. Parallel to the further development of the vocabulary this work concentrated on extracts of central aspects in grammar.

4.1. Use of markers for the rendition of single languages

For the depiction of grammatical phenomena in the integrated languages the compiled inventory proved to be sufficient on the whole. The changes in the marker inventory that resulted from the integration of the above mentioned languages have already been mentioned above (cf. chapter 3.2.3.). The development of individual KOD-lingual components made it possible to encode texts from different languages on a large scale and then to verify their comprehensibility. It became clear that the classification and arrangement of the existing markers changes depending on the nature of the source language.

This is a logical consequence of an approach which favours the flexible use of a single marker so that a single marker may represent either an inflectional ending, a prefix or a function word (preposition).

The development of different KOD-lingual components reveals in addition that in the examined languages several of the separately defined grammatical functions were frequently tightly connected to each other and that the already postulated marker bundles only cover a small part of the associations found in the languages. In principal such bundles can be represented by a combination of several markers in KOD. To what extent the establishment of further bundled markers seems to be advisable, still must be verified.

It is more essential to conclude that when comparing various KOD-lingual components with regard to the marker combinations used in different languages, fixed patterns or schemes emerge, which partially can be traced back to the typological characteristics of the examined languages. For example personal pronouns of any language will be represented in KOD with individual sequences of elements depending on whether or not case differentiations are made in this language. Moreover, for languages exhibiting the category 'gender' the inventory of required forms for encoding is different than for languages which do not exploit this category.[28]

At least for core areas in grammar it becomes possible to accelerate the integration of further languages into the system by

---

[28] The category 'grammatical gender' itself is not to be encoded (cf. also 5.1), but rather the ontological category 'gender/sex'. One consequence is that languages using grammatical gender require the differentiation of forms with respect to whether they exhibit 'gender/sex'-reference or not.

using such representation schemes because existing scheme templates can be simply transferred to new languages. However, it must be considered that the exploitation of these possibilities results in the partial limitation of the highly flexible use of markers, as they had originally been conceived.

This is because the specific position of markers in an expression can entail meanings, which are not necessarily valid when allowed to vary. For example the marker "oro" is used for the representation of an attributive determination relation between nouns.[29] In German and in English it corresponds to the adnominal genitive (Engl. *Charles' picture*, Ger. *Karls Foto* → KOD *Karloro foto*), as well as the widespread prepositional possessive, Engl. *"of"* Ger. *"von"*. (Engl. *the picture of Karl*, Ger. *das Foto von Karl* → KOD *aza foto oro Karl*) On the other hand *"oro"* is also used as a word composition element in the formation of possessive pronouns (*his picture* → *eabooro foto*).

Given such flexible use it is, however, impossible to include information in the marker which may be highly relevant for its comprehension, such as specification about the position of modifying terms or about the potential differentiation of the meanings implied.

4.2. The relation between KOD-lexemes and the vocabulary of individual languages

KOD-lexemes are defined to represent the content for which words of the basic everyday vocabulary are available in most of the languages examined. However, this does not mean that in all cases a

---

[29] This relation embraces different semantic possession relationships.

specific word of a given language can be mapped exactly to each KOD-lexeme.

On the one hand this is because KOD differentiates meanings which may to a certain extent be expressed in natural languages using superficially identical and therefore ambiguous word forms. The uniqueness of KOD-lexemes is an intrinsic principle of the system. As far as possible, ambiguous words are disambiguated upon integration into the KOD system in order to avoid potential misunderstandings for speakers of other languages.

On the other hand it must be considered that the structure of vocabulary and use of expressions in individual languages can differ fundamentally and that the KOD system must accommodate this fact. Thus the characteristic vocabulary of different languages displays different levels of differentiation:[30] a general term which is common in one language must possibly be associated to several specific terms in another language. For example, culturally established structures in one language may place emphasis on certain aspects, which seem irrelevant in the cultural domain of another language.

An example from the area of kinship terminology can make this aspect clearer:

Whereas statements regarding the family of a person in Germany, as in many other European countries as well, include an indication whether this person has brothers or sisters and if applicable how many brothers and sisters he has, this is not universally the case. In

---

[30] In the realm of bilingual lexicography one speaks of divergence and convergence between two languages in this connection. Cf. Hausmann, Franz Josef (1977): Einführung in die Benutzung der neufranzösischen Wörterbücher. Tübingen (=Romanistische Arbeitshefte 19), p. 54f.

the same context other languages must differentiate between younger and older brothers and sisters.[31] It is possible that there is no general term in the day-by-day vocabulary of this language which corresponds directly to the semantic content of the English word "brother". KOD-global includes two lexemes representing the contents 'younger brother', 'elder brother' if these two concepts are present in more than one language. A third distinct lexeme for the more general content in KOD-global will cover the usage 'brother' found in German or English.

This example demonstrates that the vocabulary of KOD-global consists of differentiated lexical units for concepts found in different languages. It is crucial to understand the relation which exists between the developed KOD-lexemes, especially if a new language must be integrated into the KOD system. To guarantee that the lexical data of the language concerned is mapped to the system in a consistent way, it is necessary to develop guidelines which explain how to deal with KOD-lexemes representing concepts that have no lexical counterpart in the given language.

Some corresponding guidelines developed for KOD distinguish the following cases:

- **rough differentiation**: a KOD-lexeme is more general than the words of a language to be integrated. In this case the KOD-lexeme can be represented in the respective language by one of several more specific terms existing in a language. Up to three of these terms can be listed.

---

[31]This is the case in Japanese for instance. For the rendition of the English term "brother" the Japanese equivalent 兄弟 kyôdai can be used with the literal meaning "sibling".

- **fine grained differentiation**: KOD-lexemes are more specifically differentiated than the words of a language to be integrated. A syntagmatic construction or a paraphrase should be entered as an equivalent; only where this evokes misunderstandings one component of the meaning must be ignored and a more general equivalent used instead.
- **partial equivalent:** The language to be integrated uses a word which might be needed in certain contexts for the representation of a KOD-lexeme, whereas in others it does not. Various cases can be differentiated: complementary distributed synonyms will both be assigned to one KOD-equivalent; semantic constraints on the usage context may be clarified by short explanations.
- **unknown concept:** rather than an equivalent an explanation must be given.

With the integration of further languages the vocabulary of KOD-global will develop into a multilinguistic resource in which the vocabulary of different languages is linked together in a special way: on the one hand ambiguous words of different languages will be disambiguated as much as possible. On the other hand this lexicon contains standardized guidelines for the treatment of cases in which equivalency relationships between languages are problematic at the level of word forms and therefore need special attention.

5. The encoding process

As already mentioned above, the use of the system encompasses two processes: the encoding and the comprehension of the encoded text. Encoding means the conversion of texts or expressions of a language into the KOD system. This process will be described in more detail in the following.

5.1. Requirements for the encoding process: KOD-lingual

The development of KOD-lingual as an extension to KOD-global is a precondition for the encoding process. KOD-lingual consists of the selection of lexemes and markers, which are used to depict an individual language, from the pool of KOD-global elements and it additionally includes the component KOD-special to embrace those phenomena not common to any other languages.

The resulting KOD-lingual-resources comprise first of all a lexicon in which the respective words of a language are mapped to KOD-lexemes and second, a manual explaining which KOD-markers are to be used for the depiction of grammatical functions in the respective language. The successful application of KOD requires the mastery of these components by the user.

With the aid of these utilities texts or expressions of the respective language can be converted into KOD-lingual.

The following example shows how.[32] To that end, a sample of those resources needed to encode an extract of a German text is

---

[32] Not all of the following literal strings have been conclusively fixed. In order to guarantee the systematic formulation of lexemes and markers certain changes may arise.

presented. These resources encompass a sample dictionary and a manual of selected grammatical functions:

Dictionary:

German	KOD-lexeme	English
sein (Verb)	put	to be
kommen	ven	to come
arbeiten	vor	to work
heute	nap	today
Ägypten	Egypt	Egypt
Regens-burg	Regens-burg	Regens-burg

Manual:

German	KOD-marker	English
ich	a	I
du	i	you
Singular. Präs. 1. Person	ana	sg. simple present. 1st person
Singular. Präs. 2. Person	ani	sg. simple present. 2nd person
in,an (Ort)	ibe	at/in
aus,von	obi	from

The dictionary registers the basic forms of content-words with their associated KOD-lexemes. The manual, on the other hand, demonstrates how function words (i.e. pronouns, prepositions) and grammatical categories (i.e. singular, simple present tense, 1st person) are to be encoded. Using these resources the following German sentences can be encoded:

German	ich	arbeite	in	Regensburg
English	*I*	*work*	*in*	*Regensburg*
KOD$_{German}$	*a*	*vorana*	*ibe*	Regensburg
German	Du	kommst	aus	Ägypten.
English	*You*	*come*	*from*	*Egypt.*
KOD$_{German}$	*i*	*venani*	*obi*	Egypt.

The development of KOD-lingual for a particular language con-stitutes a prerequisite for the encoding process: When developing the KOD-lingual component of a language it is determined which KOD-lexemes and KOD-markers are to be used to depict texts of this language. In a first step, a selection is made from the set of all KOD-global elements. Where the superficial forms of the individual language display different possible meanings, a second step must specify which meaning is being referred to in greater detail. In the above example the subscript in parentheses points out, that the German word "sein" [Engl. "to be"] is not the encoding equivalent of the German possessive pronoun "sein" [Engl. "his"] but rather the equivalent of a verb. Furthermore, the subscript to the preposition "in/at", which is to be encoded by "ibe", indicates that it is a location adjunct rather than possibly a temporal one.

The organization of reference guides for the different languages must reflect the special character of the respective language. Restrictions specific to one language determine, for example, the conventional lexicographical retrieval method for the language's vocabulary[33] for which the alphabet of the underlying language and other structural conventions must be taken into consideration.

The simple example above concentrates on the differentiation between KOD-lexemes (dictionary) and KOD-markers (manual). The starting point for encoding is not, however, the representation units of KOD but rather the respective language specific words or grammatical morphemes, which must be transposed into KOD. It is, therefore, essential to make the distinction between vocabulary and grammar in accordance to a specific individual language where encoding is concerned.

---

[33]This is not only the case concerning the macro structural level of a dictionary seen here, but also with respect to the micro structural level of lemma entries.

In languages like German in which the vocabulary can be relatively easily subdivided in different parts-of-speech, it is convenient to group the grammatical categories according to the parts-of-speech, which they feature. Combinations of person, number and tense categories, which are characteristic for German verbs, can be found in the grammatical encoding reference guide for German, for example under the topic 'verb'. Function words like pronouns, prepositions, conjunctions, etc. are to be collected in individual groups. Such function words should also be registered in the lexicon to enable quick and easy access according to the strict alphabetical order of the words in German.

Having learned KOD-global and the KOD-lingual extensions for the language to be converted such guidelines should become superfluous, especially when computer assisted "tools" come into play.

Beyond encoding instructions for specific linguistic forms a reference guide must also explain those general guidelines and principles for a language which must be followed when transposing languages into KOD in general or into a certain language type.

Such principles or guidelines pertain to grammatical phenomena, amongst others, which may only be structurally important, however, and as such do not yield any valuable information or can even be misleading for speakers of other languages. In German the category "gender" is functional, but not in the KOD-representation. German nouns are divided into different classes, for example as male, female and neuter. Here the principle applies once again that the respective sub-categorizations of the nouns should not be depicted and therefore encoded. In a similar vein, one guideline determines that case markings are to be omitted on nouns following a preposition. Exactly which case prepositions assign to an object by valency is specific to the grammar of an individual language and the meaning of the respective case cannot be treated uniformly.

5.2. Encoding and language comparison

With the exception of constraints resulting from such principles the encoding process portrays, for the most part, a structurally accurate transposition of the respective source language and therefore makes the differences visible which exist between the different languages represented in KOD.

The content of the phrase "The Arabic language is difficult" will, for instance, be encoded according to the respective source language as follows:

KOD$_{German}$	aza	arabikube	tokimova	putane	turudik
KOD$_{English}$	ivi	arabikube	tokimova	putane	turudik
KOD$_{Arabic}$	ivitokimara	arabikude		[...]	turudikubi
KOD$_{Hungarian}$	ivi	arabikube	tokimara	[...]	turudik
KOD$_{Russian}$	[...]	arabikube	tokimara	[...]	turudik
KOD$_{Chinese}$	[...]	arabiktokim		[...]	turudik

Table 3: Encoding in comparison

arabik$_{(Verb)}$	Arabic
put	to be$_{(verb)}$
tokim	language
turudik	difficult

aza	definite article$_{(def+sing.+subj).}$ [34]
ivi	*the* definite article$_{(def)}$ [35]
ube	attributive use, preceeding
ude	attributive use, following
ubi	adjective, predicative use
ova	singular
ara	singular+subject
ane	sg. simple present. 3rd pers.

In comparison the differences in the encoded languages can be clearly seen. The definite article in Arabic is prefixed to the noun. In languages like Russian and Chinese the article is missing completely. Moreover, only in German and English is there a linking-verb like "to be" which combines with the following adjective to form the predicate of the sentence. Furthermore the grammatical information associated with the definite article, the noun or the adjective is not identical in the above-listed languages.

---

[34] *aza* represents the definite article as used in German for example, where the functions denoting 1. definite, 2.singular and 3.subject congruence are all indicated in a context of grammatical opposition.

[35] *ivi* represents the form of the definite article found in English and Arabic amongst other languages, which is indifferent to distinctions for number or subject congruence.

5.3. Possibilities of encoding with computer support

Switching over from simple examples to complex sentences and larger texts the question quickly arises whether beyond the fundamental possibility of word for word encoding by someone who masters KOD a more comfortable and less complex form of automatic, or at least partially automatic, encoding is feasible.

Inasmuch as the process of automatic speech recognition establishes those grammatical categories which need to be encoded, such processes may indeed be considered helpful. Because the requirements for an automatic analysis differ considerably in different languages, individual processes must be developed and evaluated for each language.

In any case regulations must be implemented which derive from some of the above mentioned encoding guidelines. (Cf. chapter 5.1.)

In principle the approach of the KOD system implies – as described above – that encoding is not only based on surface structural words or expressions but rather on the meanings transmitted by the words or the functions connected with grammatical forms.

The success of recognition mechanisms for them is highly dependent on context features. Such context features may be taken into consideration in the process of speech recognition but they transcend the range of conventional speech recognition processes.

Therefore it is quite unlikely that encoding can ever be fully automated. It can, however, be simplified by offering the encoder automatically generated lists of the possibilities available. The user must then decide which form of encoding suits the given context.

Such support for automatic language processing has not yet been furnished. Instead the eufo-institute is concentrating on a simpler solution by which the user interactively guides the generation of proposal lists. In this case the user must decide what part-of-speech and/or syntactic function must be encoded for the elements of the text. A first prototype of a respective encoding module should be available by the end of the year 2008. Statements about the efficiency of such an "interactive" approach are not possible at present.

6. Comprehensive understanding / reception

Texts encoded from different languages provide the basis of comprehension for all those who have learned KOD-global and can use the system properly. The reception of encoded texts will be examined in detail in the following.

6.1. Verification by computer simulation

Computer software has been developed at the eufo-institute in order to check the consistency of the recently collected data and the respective degree of its comprehension. It offers the possibility to automatically transpose the version of a text represented in KOD into the integrated languages and to thereby verify to which extent encoded texts can be understood on this basis. It may also show that additional explanations of the structure of the individual language are needed.

The automatic conversion offers, at the same time, a simple introduction to the use of the system and opens the possibility to those who have not yet learned the KOD-inventory to benefit from the system at least as a recipient.

How this component is included in the architecture of KOD is shown shaded in the following diagram:

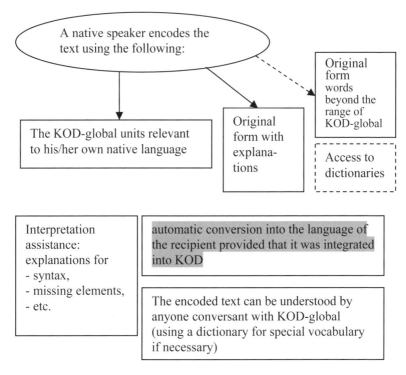

Diagram 6: Conversion of encoded texts in one of the integrated languages

The computer simulation contains an input area for the encoded text. Before processing, it must be determined from which language the text was transferred and into which target language the text should be transported.

When encoding the previously mentioned German sentence *Ich arbeite in Regensburg* may, for example, be formulated as a literal translation in different languages as follows:

German	ich	arbeite	in	Regensburg
KOD$_{German}$	*a*	*vorana*	*ibe*	Regensburg

Arabic	انا	اعمل	في	ريجينزبورج

Chinese	我	工作	在	雷根斯堡

English	I	work am working	in	Regensburg

Russian	я	работаю	полож (в, на)	Регенсбург

Hungarian	én	dolgozom	-ban, -ben	Regensburg

Diagram 7: Conversion of an encoded German sentence

This demonstrates how a recipient with a relationship to different languages may read the content of that sentence.

The examples demonstrate how much mental performance and combinational acuity each recipient must apply. The conversion does not produce a grammatically correct sentence in many cases: this conversion merely provides the representation of the encoded sentence using the resources of another language, as far as this is possible.

Differences between languages can be seen on one hand in the area of word order. On the other hand it is possible that more than one equivalent may be allocated to encoded word forms of another language. Such allocations refer to different rendition possibilities from which one must be chosen according to the context. These choices occur where in the chosen target language a differentiation is common but unknown in the source language (cf. work/am working) or where several equivalent forms might be assigned to one KOD-marker or one KOD-lexeme, which do not essentially differ in respect to the represented meaning. (complementarily distributed synonyms; cf. *in, at*)

6.2. Supplementary interpretation assistance

Where the structure of the source language and consequently its encoding differs strongly from that of the recipient additional interpretation assistance is necessary.

If need be, it can be consulted through a list of topics as shown below:

Interpretation assistance: **Arabic – English** • missing conjunction ‚and' • **sentence initial finite verb** •	**Sentence initial finite verb** Verbs at the beginning of a sentence: In Arabic there are the so-called verbal clauses starting with a verb, which constitute normal declarative sentences. What to do: think of the verb placed before the direct object.

Diagram 8: Example for interpretation assistance

The extent to which explanations are deemed necessary is dependent upon both the rules valid for the language of the recipient and how far they deviate from the rules of the encoded language.

The way encoded texts of a particular language can be converted into English for example will be shown in the first sentences of an Arabic fairy tale. The following information is given for each Arabic sentence for the purpose of explanation:

- its representation in KOD
- the rendition of the encoded sentence in an English approximation or an English explanation of the KOD-forms used
- an English translation

Arabic: كان فأر صغير يعيش مع والديه في الغابة

KOD: Ita habibaja minishude sotateevo asu mapameoro ibe ivitarova.

English equivalents: placeholder verb - represents the auxiliary verb in compound constructions || a mouse || small (used as an attribute following the reference noun) || was living (aspect 'ongoing') || with, along with, together with || his/her/its parents, parents of his/hers/it || in, at (in the city, at the university, etc.) || the woods, the forest (overt singular).

English: A small mouse lived with its parents in the woods.

Arabic وفي يوم من ايام الربيع ترك الفأر جحره ، وخرج الى الغابة مبكرا .

KOD: Tet ise yoruva ubu yorove ivihafunaro fegate ivihabibara bibahareeoro tet pamate ibi ivitarova ferite.

and || at (in/on)(i.e. at the time, in winter, in January, on a day, in the evening) ||, a day (indefinite reference) || (a part of) of (partitive) || days || of spring, the spring's || left || the mouse || his/her/its burrow || and || went | to, in, at, into (i.e. to Rome, in the city, at school, into the stadium) || the woods, the forest (overt singular)|| early.

English: And on a day of those days of spring the mouse left its burrow and went into the woods early.

Arabic أخذ الفأر معه شبكة صغيرة ليصطاد فيها الفراش .

KOD: Metate ivihabibara asueato gutaje minishude ekokimufi ibee ivihazahere.

English equivalents: Took || the mouse || with, along with, together with || a net || small (used as an attribute following the reference noun)) || in order to possibly catch (modal compound) || in him/her/it || the butterflies (overt plural direct object).

English: The mouse took a small net along in order to possibly catch the butterflies in it.

The number of explanations necessary to correctly identify and understand an encoded sentence of another language depends on the relation of both languages to each other and on the language type to which they belong. The alternative use of these explanations is guided by the linguistic knowledge the recipient already possesses.

Definite and indefinite articles are, for instance, generally not used in the Russian language. These articles have to be added by the English recipient himself in case he wants to transfer an encoded text from Russian into the English language, cf.

Russian: Празднование Нового года у древних народов совпадало с началом возрождения природы, как правило в марте.

KOD_{RUSS}: Besyukara Tinube kudaro acho paronube pabifove terunonuate asu hatim renimimaro sosenaro, ire norm ise mart.

English equivalents: Celebration-(singular+subject) ‖ New Years' party-(singular+possessive), of New Years' Eve‖ by, at, among‖ old-(attribute) ‖ peoples ‖ co-occurred‖ with, along with, together with ‖ beginning ‖ reawakening (singular+possessive)‖of nature, nature's-(singular+possessive).

English: The celebration of New Years' Eve among **the** old peoples coincided with **the** beginning of **the** reawakening of nature.

A further example:

Chinese is an isolating non-inflecting language and provides practically no morphological indication for the structural combination of words in a sentence. Attributes are often marked by the function word 的 (represented in KOD with the marker *ide*) and associated with a certain noun. A Chinese attribute is generally located to the left of the expression it modifies, irrespective of whether that expression is an adjective, noun, pronoun or a phrase. In English different forms for rendition must be chosen for the different cases: whereas in English an attributive adjective on the left side is a common occurrence as well, a corresponding attribute relation expressed by a noun or pronoun introduced by the preposition *of* is always placed to the right the reference word. Longer phrases are generally realized as relative clauses.[36] In general English attributes or attribute phrases following a reference expression are quite common which would conflict with the basic tendency in Chinese. The respective interpretation aids in English should reflect this.

In Chinese neither pronouns, nouns nor verbs are morpho-syntactically marked. Therefore an English recipient of texts encoded from Chinese must decide himself which form is appropriate for the rendition of a text or expression.

Repeated contact with sentences encoded from Chinese leads to practice in the comprehension of the above mentioned special features:

For example the following phrases show how texts encoded from Chinese can be converted into English:

Chinese: 我的孩子,
KOD: *an ide bim*
English equivalent: *I, me, mine* || preposed attribute || child
English literally: *child of 'mine'* → *my child*

Chinese: 阿拉伯语 难
KOD: *arabiktokim turudik.*
English equivalent: *Arabic difficult*
English: Arabic is difficult or: The Arabic language is difficult

---

[36] These alternative interpretations are to be explained to the English user by the above mentioned interpretation aids.

After a short training period, however, a skilled user will quickly succeed in understanding complex sentences encoded from Chinese and be able to transfer them into English. The following example summarizes the comprehension process of the above mentioned combinations in a coherent context:

Chinese: 你的大学入学考试就要到来,我猜你正忙于准备, 情绪紧张。

KOD: In ide universitetnoyansugen hon ven, an gofab in yar sisog napepag, kibom teron.

English equivalents: you, your‖ preposed attribute ‖ entrance examination for the university‖ soon, shortly‖ come‖ I, me, my‖ guess‖ you, your‖ just‖ busy (with something) ‖ prepare, preparations, ‖ mood‖ nervous.

English: Your entrance examination for the university is coming soon. I guess that you are just busy with the preparations and that you are nervous.

6.3. Learning to interact with KOD – learning KOD

The examples mentioned show how KOD works and illustrate the way the recipient or user approaches encoded texts from other languages.

In the case that the languages of the encoder and the recipient are very different from each other the text will also seem 'strange' to the recipient. Encoding does not represent a translation. It only represents the content of a text as it exists in the source language and therefore only offers the necessary foundation for comprehension by the recipient.

The approach of the KOD system – as described above – aims to structurally represent a sentence of a given language as accurately as possible. This excludes adaptations designed to explain details in a specific target language. Only under this condition is the flexible use of the system guaranteed for the depiction of any possible language, which has been integrated.

However, the encoded text and the associated explanations provide the recipient with the necessary aids for comprehension. This assistance encompasses the background knowledge necessary to deal with encoded sentences of a language which is structurally different from the recipient's language in a fundamental way. This can be seen in the examples above. Let us consider the encoding of the first Arabic sentence shown above as an example and its English equivalents:

KOD: Ita habibaja minishude sotateevo asu mapameoro ibe ivitarova.

English equivalents-: placeholder verb - represents the auxiliary verb in compound constructions || a mouse || small (used as an attribute following the reference noun) || was living (aspect 'ongoing') || with, along with, together with || his/her/its parents, parents of his/hers/it || in, at (in the city, at the university, etc.) || the woods, the forest (overt singular).

English: A small mouse was living with its parents in the woods.

The information communicated through the encoding process results in different specific insights for the comprehension of the ensuing English sentence. They are

- instructions for the modification of serialization, for example "used as an attribute following the reference noun"

- list of alternative possibilities for rendition from which one must be chosen depending on the context, for example *"in"*, *"at"*

- signals about function elements which may be ignored when being rendered in the recipient's own language, for example "placeholder verb - represents the auxiliary verb in compound constructions"[37]

The recipient must learn to effectively apply this information, evaluate it and to consult additional interpretation assistance for questions that remain open.

A repeated use of the system for the reception of texts from different languages will quickly acquaint the recipient with the respective recurring KOD-markers and their implementation. The meanings of the KOD-lexemes will easily be progressively memorized.

The extensive exploitation of the possibilities which KOD offers as a means of communication requires advanced and deeper knowledge of the representation elements of KOD-global, which arise from frequent use, as well as experience in using these representational elements in different languages. From the onset KOD was created to keep the learning effort manageable.

KOD-markers and KOD-lexemes are, for example, composed transparently so that meaning equivalencies between formally different elements of different languages become strikingly visible at many points. Additionally, KOD represents possibly irregular forms of a language in a purely regular way. Consequently the memorization of irregular forms and exception rules is avoided.

KOD is conceived in a way that when using the system two learning processes run parallel to each other. One of them refers to the communicative message and the information it contains; the

---

[37] The Arabic sentence contains an analytical verb form. In KOD person, number, tense and aspect are encoded on the verb root. For the comprehension of the encoded text the given auxiliary verb which bears the finite inflection of the predicate in the source sentence can therefore be ignored.

other refers to the linguistic structure which is mapped in KOD and its relation to the linguistic structure patterns which the recipient already knows. The use of KOD consequently combines the message and its structure with the extension and refinement of linguistic knowledge.

6.4. Further functions

Within the described computer simulation specific methods for processing and information storage are foreseen for sub-components of the system – according to the general concept for KOD described in chapter 2.

An independent lexicon module contains, for example, explanations for elements, which represent phenomena of individual languages and therefore are considered a part of KOD-lingual-special. Because in KOD-global no means of representation for these elements exist they are included in the encoded text as written in the original language (or in a Roman transcription). But in this case they also receive a special marking to distinguish them as a unit of the source language. Explanations are available for these marked elements if need be.

Words, which do not belong to the range of KOD-lingual-special, can also be portrayed in their original form, for example, proper names or internationally widespread words. The possibility of including an expression in the original form or - where applicable - in its transliterated form can also be used when the source text to be encoded needs a word which has no rendition as a KOD-lexeme. The recipient must, in this case, consult available dictionaries.

7. Possible applications of KOD

The globalization process, the growth of mobility and international cooperation stemming from political complexity within the global community, communication and the exchange of information for many different languages all assume an increasingly significant role. Concrete possibilities for the application of the developed system are, in principal, conceivable everywhere communication transcends language barriers. This is all the more the case due to the above mentioned factors which are on the rise in the realms of politics, economy, science and tourism amongst others.

The application scenarios described below in detail should only be thought of as examples.

7.1. International correspondence via email

The KOD system could well be used, for example, in email-correspondence.

Due to the speed with which any recipient can be reached worldwide electronic forms of exchange have already supplanted many conventional forms for the transmission of messages.

Anywhere that information must be exchanged quickly between speakers of different languages, for example, in the internal communication between international groups of companies, KOD offers the possibility to communicate directly without a detour through a mediating relay language which is possibly not truly mastered by either dialog partner.

The use of KOD can be attractive for those people who only partially master written English and for those people who prefer an alternative solution.[38]

The prerequisites for such use on the part of the communicator are both comfortable tools furnished for encoding, the use of which is easy to learn, and the mastery of those principals which must be followed when encoding one's own language.

The party using KOD as a recipient or receiver of a message profits from the automatic conversion of encoded messages if he is not yet thoroughly familiar with KOD-global. He must, however, still be ready to deal with possibly existing discrepancies in languages that have been encoded.

7.2. A model for many languages

The KOD-global component provides an inventory of representation elements for the depiction of different languages. For those who master this inventory encoded texts of any language become understandable.

In the computer simulation which is used for the transposition into KOD-global it is foreseen that the languages to be integrated assign possible equivalents or explanations of their language to the representation elements of KOD-global. This means that encoded

---

[38] Thomas Schneider also argues against the position that it is sufficient to rely on English for international use: [translation of quote "It would be a mistake to assume that one could restrict oneself to a supposedly global language of commerce like English. First of all it would conflict with national intentions in many lands to replace this 'colonial language' with a national language. Secondly one may not overestimate the general level of foreign language competence."] Schneider, Thomas (2000): Globalisierung – Kulturelle und sprachliche Aspekte der internationalen Zusammenarbeit. In: Wilss, Wolfram (ed.) (2000), p. 134.

texts can be converted into any of the already integrated languages. Provided that the source languages do not display any extreme idiosyncrasies, which need special explanations through an interpretation aid, the system does thereby make the encoded texts available for all integrated languages and is in no way limited to only a few of them.

This multilingual approach of the KOD system is especially interesting for users who would like to prepare a text as economically as possible for speakers of different languages. When compared to classical two-language-translation solutions or even common relay-language solutions the economical advantage of KOD is obvious. Many redundant costs drop away when a central encoded form is available.

Conceivable areas would be tourist information, manuals, product documentation and similar sectors in which the necessity for multilingual processing of information is more the rule than an exception.

In the case that mastery of KOD-global can be assumed for the addressee one must only encode the message to be transmitted. This message is then available to the addressees of different languages who master KOD.

As an alternative, encoded texts can also be used as a template for translations in different languages. The translator who knows KOD-global acts as a mediator between a multitude of languages for the addressee who does not have any KOD-knowledge at his disposal.

In contexts often dealing with similar contents, where the consistent representation of the content is important for the dissemination in several languages, a multilingual system like KOD can help guarantee the consistent quality of the respective translations.

7.3. Multilingual information retrieval

When texts of different languages exist in encoded form they are available for all speakers who have learnt KOD. KOD thereby permits a largely unfiltered and authentic view on the underlying source text.

At a sufficient level of mastery KOD can serve well to communicate the contents of sophisticated or even literary texts as seen the Arabic tale of the mouse, above.

Whether events are covered by the local press of a foreign language becomes simple to determine. How companies, foreign countries, political measures and other events are covered in the press can be illuminated just as easily.

However, texts which might be interesting for a single person must then be available in encoded form. To this end it is necessary to more closely investigate the possibilities for the support of automatic encoding.

The encoding process should consequentially be easy and quick so that the conversion of texts into KOD can quickly develop into a self-evident standard.

The utility of KOD and its chances for implementation will also be determined by alternative concepts which already exist in the area of computer assisted translation. For this reason the following chapter will deal with this topic in more detail.

8. KOD use and computer support

Presently most approaches claiming to overcome the barriers between languages favour automated solutions. It is possible to differentiate between systems which propose to produce a completely automatic translation from one language into another and systems which merely intend to assist and accelerate human translation.[39]

8.1. Fully automated translation software

The reaction to fully automated translation software, often found in public media, is somewhat contradictory. Euphoric reports of success concerning certain approaches or projects[40] are counter-balanced by more sceptical evaluations and the recognition of deficiencies where the effectiveness of contemporary software has been effectively tested with concrete examples.[41]

Fundamental statements about the status of automatic translation programmes do indeed seem controversial. Topical surveys resultantly differentiate, on the one hand, between commercial and non-commercial systems, some of which are accessible in the internet, and on the other hand, between specialized and non-specialized systems. Further criteria are performance capacity and evaluation characteristics for use like system portability and integration

---

[39] Cf. Zimmermann, Harald H. (1997), p. 1: The distinction made here is not always identical with common use. Such software is indeed also used to assist translation.

[40] Cf. Harald Schumann:"Bye, bye. Babel. Alex Waibel ist dabei, einen Menschheitstraum wahr zu machen: Er baut eine Maschine zur Überwindung aller Sprachbarrieren. In: www.Tagesspiegel.de/zeitung/Die-Dritte-Seite;art705,1888034 vom 30.12.2006

[41] Cf. "Tollmetscher?" in: Computerbild 10/2008 (28.04.2008) p. 60-64

interfaces for translation systems in differing application environments.

It is evident that fully automatic processes yield the best results when applied to specialized applications, best seen in the area of technical documentation. Language or text input can be regulated here or at least its level of complexity may be restricted. Nevertheless, quality control checks and editorial review of such automatic translation remain unavoidable.

Dedicated translation systems must be developed for specific language pairs and are not even bi-directional. The development of such systems is elaborate and expensive, and therefore often inaccessible for exactly those languages that are needed.[42]

The evaluation of available translation systems is a complex undertaking. This is all the more true when beyond the criteria of translation quality[43] criteria like end-user utility and flexibility are considered. The majority of these evaluation surveys contend that a large scale improvement of human translation performance can result from automatic translation systems.[44] At the same time such system evaluations make it clear that especially for non-professional users the training costs are frequently under-estimated and that performance expectations are usually exaggerated.

8.2 Translation Memory

In many descriptions of the field of automatic translation the consensus is that the lexicon must be considered one of the most

---

[42] Zimmermann, Harald H. (1997), p 4.

[43] Cf. Volk, Martin (2002), p. 8; Wikipedia: Maschinelle Übersetzung, p. 3 http://de.wikipedia.org/wiki/Maschinelle_Übersetzung, (last modified on 23 May 2008)

[44] Zimmermann, Harald H. (1997), p. 2; Volk, Martin (2002), p. 8

critical areas, if not the most critical. This applies to both quantative and qualitative aspects:

It is quantitatively very hard to achieve a level of coverage considered satisfactory when considering very diverse usage perspectives. The coverage level must be far higher than originally estimated.[45]

Quality demands derive from the fact that not only the special vocabulary and expert terminology of a particular discipline must be considered, but beyond that common company- or enterprise-wide terminology and naming conventions must also be taken into account.

At a fundamental level the lexica of translation systems must all be standardized in order to yield acceptable results.[46]

For this very reason most automatic translation software includes storage modules with which the currently processed vocabulary can be extended to include user-defined additions covering specific requirements. The possibility to make corrections or modify existing terminology mappings is often a part of this component.

Such modules not only exist as part of automatic translation systems but they also exist as autonomous aids with which the equivalence relationships between languages may be captured. The respective collections grow incrementally based on their use in previous translations and greatly accelerate the translation process by relieving the translator of repeated routine operations.

---

[45] One of the chief complications of translation systems dwells in the production of a lexicon with sufficient volume and quality. (cf. Zimmermann, Harald H. (1997), p. 7; Walker, Donald E./ Zampolli, Antonio/ Calzolari, Nicoletta: Introduction. In: Walker, Donald E./ Zampolli, Antonio/ Calzolari, Nicoletta (eds.) 1995, Oxford: University Press 1995, p. 2)

[46] Zimmermann, (1997), p. 7

Memory systems are not only useful as mere translation aids which translators can refine on their own for their own use. They are repositories containing networked multi-lingual equivalences for stabilized text collections that serve as a basis to generate further translation proposals for any new texts.[47]

The full potential resulting from the combination of such utilities with automatic translation software is by no means foreseeable at present.

The flexibility in design and fine tuning, which such applications offer the user, make them particularly attractive for professional translators. Some of these features might prove to be very fruitful complements to the general architecture of KOD but the level at which they will not yet overtax a KOD-user must first be empirically determined.

8.3 KOD as an element in partially automatic language transformation

KOD was developed as a system for the notation of diverse languages based exclusively on human competence and must therefore be learned.

The automatic, computer assisted rendition of KOD expressions in the language of the recipient is therefore merely an aid. It introduces and simplifies the use of the system because the incomplete mastery of KOD-lexemes and KOD-markers is no longer such a barrier. Nevertheless, the basic transparent architecture of the developed system remains simple and easy for non-experts to master.

---

[47] Statistical approaches to translation systems are also based on the analysis of available parallel text corpora.

Due to the fact that KOD is tuned for 'general' use, it will not reach the same performance levels that specialized software will achieve for well defined translation fields. However, KOD does not aspire to produce complete translation of foreign language texts and is not comparable to computer assisted translation approaches in this respect.

KOD is directed towards the user who wants to extend his capacity to exchange or research information spontaneously, at the spur of the moment and without the restriction of specific topics or languages. This wider range of comprehension has the highest priority and the recipient can therefore dispense with a detailed translation reflecting all the grammatical conventions of his mother tongue. If he would like to have an adequate translation of the text in question the professional KOD-user will still be confronted with the same formulation complications that a two-language translator encounters.

KOD will also be interesting for users who not only want to inform themselves about the contents of a foreign language text, but also for those harbouring curiosity and openness about the mechanism of language notation.

The potential for supporting the encoding process with the help of automated user-friendly components is presently being explored. (Cf. chapter 5.2.)

9. Perspectives

The point of departure for the explicated communications system KOD is highly innovative. The function as an auxiliary method and means of international communication is decisively achieved by retaining the structural integrity of the source language. This structure is made transparent by presenting KOD-markers and KOD-lexemes in a way that users without linguistic training can quickly understand them.

This approach works in conjunction with construction principles which are far more transparent than the mechanisms and theory behind all automatic translation systems. These systems generally include different modules and are customized to automatically overcome a complex series of dedicated tasks.

KOD - in stark contrast - offers people without foreign language experience, those who do not consciously master any foreign language, the possibility to discover and unlock the contents of expressions or texts originating in a foreign language. At the same time the process of encoding one's own mother tongue and the comprehension of previously encoded texts or expressions from other languages promote inherent language competence, because it easily deals with diverse linguistic structures and is no longer restricted by the barriers of pronunciation and orthography in a foreign language.

Such empowerment may well take on a decisive role as a core competency in the face of progressing globalization.

Because the KOD system is not a stand-alone construction but rather a complement to an individual native language it fortifies the importance of such an existing language and contributes to the preservation of language diversity.

Without human involvement in the process of encoding and a certain conviction to learn the basics on the part of the recipient KOD will not possibly work.

As described above the inventory of KOD-global was compiled on the basis of a broad selection of phenomena from 15 different languages belonging to different language types and language families. Specific components of the KOD-lingual notation for grammatical functions in parts of selected languages were produced with which the particular formal aspects of these languages can be usefully rendered.

Presently the data compiled is being verified and prepared for the integration in a computer assistance application. The application will encompass further features by the end of the year including a module supporting the process of encoding.

A summarization reviewing the results of all previous development is in preparation.

Bibliography

Bickel, Balthasar/Nichols, Johanna (2007): Inflectional morphology. In: Shopen, Timothy (ed.) (2007, 2nd ed.), volume 3, p. 169-240

Bodmer, Frederick (2004): Die Sprachen der Welt. Geschichte – Grammatik – Wortschatz in vergleichender Darstellung. Köln: Parkland Verlag (Eng. original „The Loom of Language", translated by Rudi Keller)

Baerman, Matthew/ Brown, Dunstan (2005a): Case Syncretism. In: Haspelmath, Martin et al. (eds.): The World Atlas of Language Structures. Oxford: Oxford University Press, p. 118- 121.

Baerman, Matthew/ Brown, Dunstan (2005b) Syncretism in Verbal Person/ Number Marking. In: Haspelmath, Martin et al. (eds.) (2005): The World Atlas of Language Structures. Oxford: Oxford University Press, p. 122-125.

Bußmann, Hadumod (ed.) (2002): Lexikon der Sprachwissenschaft. 3. aktualisierte und erweitere Aufl. Stuttgart: Kröner Verlag

Campbell, G.L. (2000): Compendium of the World's Languages. London/New York: Routledge, 2nd ed.

Comrie, Bernard (1981^1; 1989^2): Language universals and linguistic typology: Syntax and morphology. Oxford: Blackwell, 2. facsimile 1995

Comrie, Bernard (1985/2000): Tense. Cambridge: University Press, (7th ed.)

Croft, W. (1993): Typology and universals. Cambridge: University Press, 2nd ed. (=Cambridge textbooks in linguistics)

Crystal, David (1997): The Cambridge Encyclopedia of Language. 2nd ed. Cambridge: University Press

Finegan, Edward (1990): English. In: Comrie, Bernard (ed.): The World's Major Languages. New York/Oxford: Oxford University Press, p. 77-109

Glück, Helmut (ed.) (2000): Metzler Lexikon Sprache. Zweite, überarbeitete u. erweiterte Aufl. Stuttgart/Weimar: Metzler Verlag

Hausmann, Franz Josef (1977): Einführung in die Benutzung der neufranzösischen Wörterbücher. Tübingen (=Romanistische Arbeitshefte 19)

Jakobson, Roman (1959): On Linguistic Aspects of Translation. In: Brower, R.A. (ed.) On Translation, Cambridge, MA, Harvard University Press, p. 232-239.

Jespersen, Otto (1924/1992): The Philosophy of Grammar. Chicago and London: The University of Chicago Press 1992.

Klein, Horst G./Stegmann, Tilbert D. (2000): EuroComRom – Die sieben Siebe: Romanische Sprachen sofort lesen können. Aachen: Shaker Verlag

Landau, Sidney I. (1984/1993): Dictionaries. The Art and Craft of Lexicography. Cambridge: University Press, 3rd ed.

The Leipzig Glossing Rules: Conventions for interlinear morpheme-by-morpheme glosses. 'Revised 2008. URL: http://www.eva.mpg.de/lingua/resources/glossing-rules.phg

Maas, Utz (1999): Phonologie. Opladen/Wiesbaden: Westdeutscher Verlag

Phillipson, Robert (2000[5]): Linguistic Imperialism. Oxford: Oxford University Press

Phillipson, Robert (2003): English-Only Europe? Challenging Language Policy. London/New York: Routledge

Sakaguchi, Alicja (1998): Interlinguistik. Gegenstand, Ziele, Aufgaben, Methoden. Frankfurt a. Main: Peter Lang (= Duisburger Arbeiten zur Sprach- und Kulturwissenschaft; vol. 36)

Schneider, Thomas (2000): Globalisierung: Kulturelle und sprachliche Aspekte der internationalen Zusammenarbeit. In: Wilss (ed.) (2000), p. 129-138.

Schumann: Bye, bye, Babel. In: www.Tagesspiegel.de 12 Dec 2006

Schwanke, Martina (1991): Maschinelle Übersetzung. Ein Überblick über Theorie und Praxis. Berlin/ Heidelberg/ New York: Springer-Verlag.

Shopen, Timothy (ed.) (2007, 2nd ed.): Language typology and syntactic description. vol. 3: Grammatical categories and the lexikon. Cambridge: University Press

Tollmetscher? In: Computerbild 10/2008 28 April 2008, p. 60-64

UNGEGN publicity brochure. In the internet as: http:/www.unstats.un.org/unsd/ geoinfo/about_us_html

Vielberth, Johann: An Idea for an International System of Communication. In: Vielberth, Johann/ Drexel, Guido (eds.) (2003): Linguistic Cultural Identity and International Communication. Maintaining Language Diversity in the Face of Globalization. Saarbrücken: AQ Verlag, p. 9-16

Vielberth, Johann (2006): Das System KOD. Überlegungen zur Idee, Gestaltung und zu Chancen eines sprachübergreifenden Verständigungsmittels. Regensburg: Institut für Entwicklung und Forschung Dr. Vielberth e.K.

Volk, Martin (2002): Das Evaluieren von Software für die maschinenunterstützte Übersetzung. In: Technische Dokumentation (2002). In the internet as: http://www.doku.net/artikel/dasevaluie.htm

Walker, Donald E./ Zampolli, Antonio/ Calzolari, Nicoletta: Introduction. In. Walker, Donald E./ Zampolli, Antonio/ Calzolari, Nicoletta (eds.) 1995, Oxford: University Press 1995, p. 1-19

Wikipedia: Maschinelle Übersetzung, http://de.wikipedia.org/wiki/Maschinelle_Übersetzung, last updated 23 May 2008

Wilss, Wolfram (ed.) (2000): Weltgesellschaft -
Weltverkehrssprache – Weltkultur. Internationale Tagung
der Europäischen Akademie in Otzenhausen/Saarland 1999,
Tübingen: Stauffenberg Verlag

Zaefferer, Dietmar (1998): Deskriptive Grammatik und Sprachver-
gleich. Tübingen: Max Niemeyer (=Linguistische Arbeiten;
vol. 383)

Zimmermann, Harald H. (1997): Maschinelle Übersetzung. In: Buder,
Rehfeld/ Seeger, Strauch (1997): Grundlagen der praktischen
Information und Dokumentation. p. 244-253, citation. URN:
urn:nbn:de:bsz:291-scidok-7417; URL: http//scidok.sulb.uni-
saarland.de/volltexte/2007/741

Index of the diagrams and tables

Diagrams

Tables

Index

Appendix

I. The inventory of the KOD-phonemes

With the exception of sign languages (for the deaf) all languages of the world consist of symbols which can be described as a combination of a limited number of sound patterns.[48] Because the writing systems employed by the world's languages are very different, only the sound patterns used by the languages can be taken as the basis for constructing a communication system which allows equal access for speakers of any language whatsoever.

I.1. Goals and material used

Seen from the perspective of the phoneme inventory, the KOD system was intended to comprise sound segments which would be easy to pronounce and recognize for the speakers of the greatest possible number of languages. As the smallest units of the system these sound segments are designed to form grammatical morphemes (=markers) and words and to phonologically mark the difference between the individual units of the system.

The first step towards determining these sound segments involved research into which sound patterns appeared most frequently in the phonological systems of languages all over the world.

The basic idea underlying this approach was that by choosing sounds that occurred frequently in many languages, the communication system KOD would be able to ensure, in terms of phonology, a higher degree of accessibility and ease of use (ease of

---

[48] In linguistics the term "double articulation" is used to describe a structural pattern of languages which is universal. The term was introduced by Martinet (1965). It refers to the fact that combination is not only relevant in the syntactic use of words, but also in their formation.

pronunciation; listening comprehension) for speakers of the greatest possible number of languages.[49]

Material pertaining to the phonological systems of 317 languages which was compiled by the UPSID Study (= University of California, Los Angeles, Phonological Segment Inventory Database) provided the basic data.[50] The UPSID Study comprises languages which have been assigned to the following language families as follows:

Language family	Identification numbers	No. of languages included
Indo-European	000-049	21
Ural-Altaic	050-099	22
Niger-Kordofanian	100-199	31
Nilo-Saharan	200-249	21
Afro-Asiatic	250-299	21
Austro-Asiatic	300-349	6
Australian	350-399	19
Austro-Tai	400-499	25
Sino-Tibetan	500-599	18
Indo-Pacific	600-699	27
Amerindian	700-899	89
Others (Dravidan, Caucasian, Khoisan, Eskimo-Aleut, etc.)	900-999	18

Table 4: Language families in UPSID[51]

---

[49] Consequently, the frequency of a phoneme was determined on the basis of how many languages the sound occurred in and not on the total number of speakers of these languages.

[50] The results of the UPSID project have been published in Maddieson, Ian (1984); Patterns of Sound. Cambridge: University Press. In addition, the Handbook of the International Phonetic Association, Cambridge: University Press 1999 was also referred to, in which 29 inventories of phonemes of different languages are listed for the purpose of illustration.

[51] Maddieson, Ian (1984): Patterns of Sounds. Cambridge/London/New York et al. Cambridge University Press, p. 159.

It covers a very wide range of the world's languages.

The sound patterns which this underlying data demonstrated to have the highest degree of dissemination were then, in a second step, subjected to a phonological evaluation. This assessment was necessary due to the fact that an inventory of sound patterns based solely on the criteria of frequency does not occur in this specific constellation in any given language. The sound patterns compiled on the basis of frequency, therefore, were also characterized by the degree of distinction in their articulation. There are distinctions which occur very frequently but do not transport differences in meaning. This must be taken into account. An example serves to clarify this point: Of the 40 sound patterns which the UPSID Study data shows to occur most frequently in the documented 317 languages, the voiceless dental-alveolar plosive ["t"] occupies position 17 in the ranking, the voiceless alveolar plosive [t] position 26 and the voiceless dental plosive [t̪] [52] position 35. The distinction in articulation between "dental-alveolar", "alveolar" and "dental" is phonologically used for the plosive in comparatively few languages, however.[53] It would not make sense, therefore, to incorporate such distinctions into the KOD communication system.

---

[52] The study referred to concentrates on sound patterns which transport a functional difference in meaning as phonemes in different languages. However, when listed according to the frequency of their occurrence, they are excluded from the inventory of phonemes as a whole. The sound patterns under scrutiny are therefore depicted here phonetically (set in square brackets). When dealing with sound patterns systematically related to each other, slashes are used.

[53] According to the calculations of R. Maier, this distinction occurs in only 29 of the 317 languages under study, i.e. 9.15 %.

With this idea in mind, a closer study was conducted to determine which articulation of the most widespread sound patterns in the languages studied, actually often transports a difference in meaning. These would, therefore, be suitable for incorporation as separate KOD phonemes.

I.2. The basic KOD phonemes

On the basis of the procedural steps enumerated above an inventory of phonemes was established for KOD which in the area of vowels consists of five units /i/,/e/,/a/,/o/,/u/ and was extended by two diphthongs /ai/ and /au/. While there are some languages that have less than five vowels (for example classical Arabic whose phoneme system only distinguishes between the three vowel units /i/,/a/ and /u/ [54]), a vowel system with five vowel units is standard for most languages and, as a rule, can be considered easy to use. [55]

For the consonants, based on the above enumerated criteria, 14 consonant phonemes were determined which can be distinguished from each other according to the articulation features as illustrated in the following table:

---

[54] Cf. Ternes, Elmar (1987), p. 161.

[55] Referring to the Spanish vowel triangle system with its three stages, Ternes, Elmar (1987), for example, postulates the following: "This is a very simple vowel system with a small number of phonemes. It is exactly this system which is widespread globally: It can be found in the different language families and in all parts of the globe, with the exception of Spanish, for example in Russian (East Europe), Swahili (Africa), Hausa (Africa), Quechula (South America,) Japanese (East Asia)." (p. 149f).

no.	phoneme	differentiating features	dissemination in the UPSID Study languages	possibilities for implementation
1	/p/	voiceless, labial, closed	90.54%	aspirated, palatalized, implosive, ejective
2	/b/	voiced, labial, closed	70.98%	aspirated, palatalized, implosive, ejective
3	/t/	voiceless, dental-alveolar, closed	99.05%	from dental to retroflex, aspirated, palatalized, implosive, ejective
4	/d/	voiced, dental-alveolar, closed	67.82%	from dental to retroflex, aspirated, palatalized, implosive, ejective
5	/k/	voiceless, velar, closed	98.11%	aspirated, palatalized, ejective
6	/g/	voiced, velar, closed	60.57%	aspirated, palatalized, implosive, ejective
7	/ʧ/	voiceless, affricate	62.46%	with fricative segments ranging from alveolar to palatal
8	/s/	voiceless, dental-alveolar, fricative	86.12%	from dental to retroflex, ejective

103

no.	phoneme	differentiating features	dissemination in the UPSID Study languages	possibilities for implementation
9	/m/	labial, nasalized, closed	94.32%	bilabial oder labiodental
10	/n/	dental-alveolar, nasalized, closed	95.90%	from dental to retroflex
11	/w/	voiced, labial, approximate	78.86%	labiodental or labiovelar
12	/j/	voiced, palatal, approximate	85.49%	approximate or voiced, palatal fricative
13	/l/	lateral, liquid	78.86%	lateral liquid
14	/h/	articulated in the glottis	64.98%	as aspirate or glottal fricative

Table 5: Set of KOD phonemes selected by frequency

Calculations based on the UPSID data indicate that all the other consonant sound patterns have a lower degree of dissemination. Nonetheless, further sound patterns can easily be integrated into this phonological system, along with the 14 basic consonant phonemes outlined above. The following additional sound patterns have been established in connection with different features which the system already makes use of for other purposes:

no.	phoneme	different features	dissemination in the UPSID Study languages
15	/ŋ/	velar, nasalized, closed	approx. 50%
16	/f/	voiceless, labial, fricative	approx. 50%
17	/ʃ/	palatal- alveolar, voiceless, fricative	approx. 50%
18	/z/	voiced, alveolar, fricative	approx. 30%
19	/x/	velar, fricative	approx. 30%
20	/dʒ/	voiced, affricate	approx. 30%

Table 6: Additional KOD consonant phonemes

These sound segments were incorporated as additional phonemes
into the KOD communication system in order to increase the possibilities for combining different sounds. The UPSID Study reaches the
conclusion that there is no single consonant segment which occurs in
all languages.[56]

Given that there is a lack of global concurrence in the phoneme
inventories of the world's languages, the phoneme inventory which
was established for KOD offers a compromise solution. It aims to
minimize problems in pronunciation for the speakers of the different
languages. Nonetheless, there is no avoiding sound segments which
do not occur in a given speaker's native language and which therefore must be learned.

In its essential elements, the KOD phoneme inventory is based on
frequency of occurrence which was calculated at the eufo-institute on

---

[56] Cf. Crystal, David (1997): The Cambridge Encyclopedia of Language, 2.
printing. Cambridge: Cambridge University Press, p. 167.

the basis of the UPSID data. The frequency studies which were implemented within the framework of the UPSID project itself can also be drawn on for comparative corroborative data.[57] Of the twenty consonant phoneme segments which the study shows as occurring most frequently, only three are not represented in the KOD inventory of phonemes. They are the sound patterns: /r/, /ɲ/ and /ʔ/.

These three sound segments were not included in the KOD inventory of phonemes due to concerns about the difficulty of learning them and the related distinctions in their articulation for the speakers of larger language families.[58]

In their place the sound patterns /z/, /x/ and /ʤ/ were substituted for inclusion in the KOD inventory of phonemes. Although these sounds do not occur quite as frequently, they are cited by Maddieson as possible candidates for an extension of the consonant inventory – beyond the most frequently occurring 20 consonants.[59] Maddieson's positive assessment of an inventory of phonemes based primarily on frequency for linguistic comparisons between different languages can apply equally to the only slightly modified KOD inventory of

---

[57] Cf. Maddieson, Ian (1984) p. 12; as well as the resume in David Crystal (1997), p. 167.

[58] An example would be the difficulties in the distinction between /r/ and /l/ in Asian languages. The glottal stop is not consciously perceived in many of the languages in which it occurs. The sound pattern /ɲ/ is not always sharply differentiated from the "n" segment which is palatalized in some languages. In some cases, however, where a proven difficulty in pronunciation for certain sound patterns could have been a reason for exclusion from the KOD system, such as the sound [h] for the speakers of certain languages (French) and the differentiation between [s] and [z], which is difficult to learn for speakers of other languages, admittedly a certain degree of arbitrariness cannot be excluded.

[59] Cf. Maddieson, Ian (1984), p. 12.

phonemes: "By simply considering frequency we obtain an inventory which is typologically most plausible in its structure. This is encouraging."[60]

I.3. Extensions and possible variations in pronunciation

Considering the possibilities for implementing the appropriate phoneme segments which were selected for the KOD system, it is clear that there is a great deal of leeway for variations of pronunciation within the inventory of those compiled phonemes.

This corresponds to a certain extent with the situation one would also encounter when speaking natural languages, where there is also a certain range of variation in the implementation of phonemes. For an international communication system which is designed to be used by speakers of different languages, it is obvious that the range of tolerance for different articulations which the phoneme system offers is a distinct advantage. Accordingly, for those languages in which certain important phonological segments of KOD do not occur, similar sound units could be tolerated as variations in the pronunciation (allophones) for a given KOD phoneme. This would correspond to the habit of those striving to learn a foreign language who – partly unconsciously – make use of sound patterns, which are familiar to them from their own native language, as substitutes for the sound forms which appear strange to them in another language.

In this sense, the voiced labiodental fricative [v], as well as the labiovelar approximate [w], could be used as a variation or allophone of the phoneme /w/.

---

[60] ibid.

Along the same line, aside from the lateral implementation of the phoneme /l/, other liquids, in particular the implementation of the /r/ sound by means of vibration, taps and trills could be allowed.

To what extent variations in the pronunciation for speakers of different native languages can be tolerated without leading to the danger of misunderstanding, however, has to be studied in greater detail and determined at a later point in time in connection with the compilation of KOD-lingual units for the KOD system. From the point of view of listening comprehension, it will certainly be necessary to draw limits for variation. Should features of articulation be concerned, which speakers of a certain language do not master, then, as is the case when learning a foreign language, the passive and active differentiation of this feature will also have to be learned in order to become conversant with KOD.

Beyond the basic KOD-global phonemes additional phonological elements will be required for the integration of international words in the KOD system.

II. Does KOD need its own special script?

Since the basic idea behind KOD is to create a communication system which is available and equally accessible to speakers of different native languages and does not place speakers of any given language or language family at a disadvantage in learning the system, the question arises, whether an independent graphology system has to be developed to uphold the idea of neutrality.

As a result of detailed deliberation the team at the eufo-institute decided to use an alphabet primarily based on the Roman characters as shown above.[61]

On the one hand it is highly questionable that the Roman alphabet is biased towards western civilisation, both with respect to its historical development and its current distribution among the languages of the world. In this vein Harald Haarmann (1994) for example expresses the opinion that the broad distribution of the Roman alphabet illustrates its extraordinary adaptability. "Das lateinische Alphabet hat sich in der Moderne als äußerst flexibles System bewährt. Ergänzt durch diakritische Zusatzzeichen ist es sogar effektiv, um eine Tonsprache wie das Vietnamesische zu schreiben."[62]

---

[61] From 2001 to 2003 an autonomous character system was developed at the eufo-institute to transcribe all KOD phonemes. It is available for future purposes.

[62] "In modern times the Latin alphabet has proved to be an extremely flexible system. When complemented with diacritical notations it is even efficient enough to transcribe a tonal language like Vietnamese." Haarmann, Harald (1994): Entstehung und Verbreitung von Alphabetschriften. (Evolution and spread of Alphabetic Scripts) In: Günther, Hartmut/Ludwig, Otto (eds.): Schrift und Schriftlichkeit. Writing and Its Use. An

On the other hand KOD is primarily concerned with the fundamental choice of a writing system, that means the decision for an alphabetic, syllabic or logographic system. In the case that this decision favors a phonologically faithful alphabetic system[63] – due to distributional dominance – that would mean a massive reorientation for all speakers of a logographically or syllabically transcribed language.

Consequentially a writing system must be used for which at least adaptation patterns already exist and with which speakers of these languages are already acquainted through foreign language acquisition. Both conditions are well satisfied by the Latin alphabetical transcription.

The linguists of the eufo-institute have decided to place more weight on this greater functional utility rather than following the occasionally proposed opinion that the use of this character system lends KOD a eurocentric bias.

---

interdisciplinary Handbook of International Research, Vol. 1, Berlin/New York: Walter de Gruyter, (=HSK, vol 10.1), p. 346.

[63] The notion of a phonologically faithful alphabetic system is used to mark the difference to a primarily morphologically orientated alphabetic system, such as English.

III. International words in KOD

III.1. Determination of a basic set

International words have been a subject of research in the philological disciplines of European languages for a long time.[64] As described above, international words in this context were generally defined as words of different languages which occur in a similar word-form (phonological and/or graphological) and which share at least one of their meanings. To be of use as a basis for the determination and analysis of international words this definition must be specified.

Depending on their different goals the contemporary linguistic approaches apply different criteria for such specification. The scope of languages which were incorporated in studies of the subject has remained restricted for a long time to correspondences between the European languages. Only of late has the focus turned to non-European languages as well.[65]

---

[64] Cf. the research summary by Kolwa, Andrea (2003): Zur Geschichte der Internationalismus-Forschung. In: Braun, Peter et al. (eds.): Internationalismen II, Tübingen: Max Niemeyer, p. 13-21 as well as: Schaeder, Burkhard (1990): Versuch einer theoretischen Grundlegung der Internationalismus-Forschung. In: Braun, Peter et al. (eds.): Internationalismen. Studien zur interlingualen Lexikologie und Lexikographie. Tübingen: Max Niemeyer, p. 34-46 and: Bergmann, Rolf (1995): 'Europäismus' und 'Internationalismus'. Zur lexikologischen Terminologie. In: Sprachwissenschaft 20 (1995), p. 239-277.

[65] The articles by Wilita Sriurangpong, Neelakshi Ch. Premawardhena and Angelika Werner in the collection by Peter Braun, Burkhard Schaeder and Johannes Volmert published in 2003 concentrate on international words in Thai, Singhalese and Japanese. Cf. Braun, Peter et al. (eds.) (2003): Internationalismen II, Tübingen: Max Niemeyer. The research of international words initiated by the editors of this volume stimulated further

The KOD communication system is designed mainly to integrate such expressions as "international words" which have achieved widespread distribution due to the importance of the things or concepts represented by these words. Similarities of word forms in different languages may however also be caused by the close historical relationship between these languages. Therefore, it is necessary to examine languages of different historical origins selecting international words not exclusively based on historical interrelationships.

In order to establish a fundamental stock of international words for the KOD system a survey was conducted at the eufo-institute from March 2003 to April 2004 based on 3,500 German and English terms. The goal was to determine the distribution of these words and to confirm their common meanings in twelve contrasting languages. The subject of the survey were those words which belong to the domain of general vocabulary and are presumably wide spread. Distribution evidence bases on reliable descriptions of word loaning processes and the competence of the multilingual experts at the eufo-institute.

As a rule of thumb the team at Regensburg postulated the distribution of a similar word-form displaying at least one identical

---

analysis, specifically the contrastive treatment of international words in Turkish and Arabic, cf. Selmy, Elsayed Madbouly (2003): Internationalismen im Arabischen – im Vergleich mit dem Deutschen. Eine empirische Studie. In: EliSe: Essener Linguistische Skripte – in digital form. year 3, volume 2, p. 7-42; Özen, Ümit (1999): Internationalismen-Konzeption einer interlexikologischen Theorie. Dargestellt am Beispiel der Ergebnisse einer empirischen Auswertung von türkischen Zeitungstexten. Diss. Siegen, <http://www.ub.uni-siegen.de/epub/diss> .

meaning in eight of the fourteen languages analyzed. This was the criterion for its incorporation as an international word in KOD-global.

The investigation also considered languages that do not use the Roman alphabet, such as Arabic, Bulgarian, Chinese, Modern Greek, Hindi, Japanese and Russian. For these languages phonological representations were used in compliance with the accepted transcription and transliteration conventions. Within this framework the survey yielded a list of 2,254 international words which fulfilled the established criteria.[66]

The list of international words includes expressions, which belong to different fields. For the most part they are

- expressions from the field of medicine: "AIDS" "allergy",
- technical terminology: "automatic", "antenna",
- terms of academic discourse: "academy", "anonymous" and
- names for consumable goods or luxury items: "champagne", "pizza", "whisky",

which have entered the day to day vocabulary of most languages. With respect to the distribution of the parts-of-speech, nouns make up by far the largest group of international words. They constitute about 80% of the list including a few nominal compounds.

There are 32 international expressions which enjoy a special status because they often occur as prefixes of terms considered to be foreign words, e.g. "mikro-", "neo-" , "trans-", "ultra-". The great majority[67] of these terms originate in Latin or ancient Greek.

In contrast to the general vocabulary of the KOD system international words may indeed have more than one meaning. There are

---

[66] This quantity refers to the number of constructed international KOD words, and not the number of meanings covered by the list.
[67] The only exception so far has been the element "top" as in "top management", "top offer", "top price", etc.

several cases of international words displaying two separate meanings, which however tend to be closely related. This can be seen in the example of the German word "Energie" 'energy' which can be used in the meaning of a) power/strength in the sense of physics or b) bodily-mental capacity in many languages: English, Bulgarian, Finnish, Modern Greek, Italian, Japanese[68], Croatian, Hungarian and derived from English in Yorùbá.

Widely distributed words that represent more than two discrete meanings do exist, but they are much more seldom. An example of this are the terms "code" and "plus". "Code" can mean a) a symbolic system, cipher, b) the internal language of computers, c) genetic information or d) a secret number as a password. "Plus" has the meanings a) additionally, b) above freezing c) the positive pole of an electronic device.[69]

III.2. Phoneme and graphic structure of international words

III.2.1. The word stem

One of the main criteria within the definition of international words is the similarity of the morphological form of these words in different languages. Strictly speaking this criterion only concerns the stem of international words, whereas suffixes characterizing the part-

---

[68] In this case the second meaning is used considerably less frequently in comparison to the Japanese word "chikara".

[69] Peter Braun points out that there are possible, even if infrequent cases of "interlingual polysemy". (cf. Braun, Peter (1999), p. 20, Internationalismen und Europäismen. Eine lexikologische Analyse. In: Sprachreport 4 (1999, p. 20-24). However not all languages possess the respective international words. Speakers of languages which display other differentiations and express the individual meanings of these international words differently, will need to decide which meaning is relevant in a particular encoded text. For the most part context is enough.

of-speech category of a word often undergo particular adaptations in the target language during the process of word loaning.[70]

Furthermore, similarity can only be related to the phonological shape of words, when languages employing completely different writing systems are taken into account, which is crucial for the project KOD. For a large part of the terms which proved to be international words in the survey, the following regularity actually seems to be valid: There are significant correspondences concerning the consonants of the words belonging to different languages. The vowels of international words, in contrast, vary to a high degree.

English plays a specific role being the most important source language. It is therefore very relevant for the distribution of international words originally belonging to other European languages as well.

Common features, which connect English and other European languages in the field of vocabulary, are visible in the more conservative domain of orthography, but not in pronunciation where

---

[70] The position maintained by Kolwa is that when considering diverse languages different patterns of grammatical endings restrict their recognition. Cf.: Kolwa, Andrea (2003b): Probleme der Bestimmung von Internationalismen im Bereich der Politik. In: Braun, Peter et al. (eds.), ibid., p. 64. Kolwa doubts "whether lexemes with incongruent prefixes or suffixes can be identified as representatives of interlexical units if the meanings of such incongruent morphemes remain unknown" („ob Lexeme mit inkongruenten Prä- und Suffixen als Vertreter interlexikalischer Einheiten zu identifizieren sind, wenn die Bedeutung dieser inkongruenten Morpheme nicht bekannt ist.") ibid.

English in several respects displays some peculiarities when compared with other European languages.[71]

There are cases in which a contrast between non-European and European languages arises, because especially non-European languages reflect the importance of English as the source and mediator of many international words.

Phonemes for the uniform depiction of international words in the KOD system could for that reason be established merely on the basis of a majority. Such phonemes were delineated for all word stems having equivalents in at least eight languages.

In addition to the pronunciation of a word used in the majority of languages under study the team in Regensburg strove to keep the phonological word form simple and to restrict them to the range of phonemes already claimed for KOD as far as possible.

Graphological conventions were implemented concerning the following phonemes or phoneme-grapheme-correspondences:

/ts/ -<c>;
/r/ - <r> versus /l/ - <l>;
/v/ - <v> versus /w/ - <w>

[dʒ] and [ʒ] are both possible pronunciations of the grapheme <j> in international words.

---

[71] However, when considering the languages of the European region Peter Braun (1990: p. 17f) makes the general observation that it is precisely at the level of pronunciation that international words diverge most. "The phonetic relationships of different languages very often help to cover up identity and similarity and permit dissimilarity to come into prominence: consider 'museum' or 'nation'." ["Die phonetischen Verhältnisse verschiedener Sprachen tragen sehr oft dazu bei, die Gleichheiten und Ähnlichkeiten geradezu zu verdecken und die Ungleichheiten in Erscheinung treten zu lassen (vgl. Museum, Nation)."] Braun, Peter (1990): Internationalismen-Gleiche Wortschätze in europäischen Sprachen. In: Braun, Peter et al (eds.) (1990) p. 13-34.

As the KOD system employs a phonologically faithful alphabetic writing system, the orthography of international words in KOD sometimes deviates from the orthography common for these words in languages using the Roman alphabet. Examples are the KOD international word „aksesoar" for German "Accessoire" [akse'soar], Engl. "accessory", the KOD international word "arkitekt" for German "Architekt" [arçi'tekt], English "architect", the KOD international word "eksotik" for German "exotisch" [e'ksotiʃ], English "exotic".

Phonologically faithful word forms are, however, much easier to recognize for speakers of languages which employ other writing systems. Empirical tests carried out at the eufo-institute have also verified that the word structure as a whole guarantees recognition especially in the case of multisyllabic words.

However, emphasizing the pronunciation when determining the orthography of a word in KOD sometimes leads to difficult and irritating word forms. That is why in exceptional cases the orthographic word form established in the majority of languages employing the Roman alphabet was chosen for KOD. It is then complemented by a pronunciation that deviates from the standard phoneme-grapheme-relation of the KOD system.

Written transcriptions like <blek aut> based on the English pronunciation for "black out" are not only an alienation problem for languages with an alphabetic script. They pose large problems for languages with non-alphabetic script, too. Especially relatively recent international words, which have not yet been completely integrated in the respective languages tend to import the English orthography along with the pronunciation (either by some process of transliteration or by the redundant use of two scripts). The attempt to do justice to those languages without an alphabetic script can, moreover, lead to formulations that are no longer recognizable in the great majority of (other) languages.

For instance an international word was established as an equivalent for the German word "Ballett" pronounced [balet]. The equivalent has the KOD script "ballet" and the pronunciation [bale]. The KOD lexeme "black out" is associated with the pronunciation [blek aut], the KOD lexeme "(blue) jeans" with the pronunciation [blu dʒins], "atelier" is pronounced [atel'je] and "brandy" [brendi].

When compared to the total number of KOD international words these exceptions only constitute a small set.

III.2.2. Derivational suffixes

The following suffixes were defined to represent word composition elements for KOD international words:

-izem: characterizing a , 'theoretical position or pathological inclination towards something' in analogy to German *-ismus*, English *-ism*, Greek *-ismos*, Russian *-izm*. A suffix with this function is widespread among many European languages:

Bulgarian:	алкохолизъм alkohol - izum	KOD-global: alkol – izem
Croatian:	alkohol -izam	
English:	alcohol – ism	
Finnish:	alkohol - ismi	
German:	Alkohol - ismus	
Greek:	αλκοολισμός alkol - ismos	
Hungarian:	alkohol – izmus	
Italian:	alcol - ismo	
Russian:	алкоголизм alkogol - izm	
Turkish:	alkol - izm	

-ir **marking verbs**: by using this suffix a certain alienation may arise for those languages, which do not use an overt verb-ending, English for instance. Verbs like English adopt (v) versus KOD "adoptir", English assist (v) versus KOD "asistir" give examples. The suffix *–ir* is not only found in German (more specifically *-ieren* derived from French and Latin templates) but also in Slavic languages such as Bulgarian *-iram*, Croatian *-irati* and Russian *-irovat"*. It is also comparable to the frequent suffix *-er* in French, the Italian suffixes *-are* or *-ere* (and often *-ire*) and *-aro* in Modern Greek. The following example shows this KOD-global standardization.

Bulgarian:	документи́рам dokument - iram	KOD-global: dokument - ir
Croatian:	dokument – irati	
English:	document [dɒkjumənt]	
Finnish:	dokument - oida	
German:	dokument - ieren	
Hungarian:	dokument – ál	
Italian:	document - are	
Russian:	документировать dokument – irovat'	

-ik **as suffix for adjectives**, related to German *-isch*, English *-ic*, French: *-ique*, Turkish *-ik*, Japanese *-ikku*, Greek *-i/aikos*, Italian: *-ico/-ica*. Particular suffixes for adjectives also occur in the languages Finnish *–inen, -isti* in Croatian *–ski, -ni* and Russian with the suffixes *-ičeskij* and *–nyj*. The intention to establish a regular pattern for KOD international words led to the decision to use the suffix *-ik* as a unique characterization for widespread adjectives, including those which already contain an adjective marking as *-al, -iv/f*.

119

Arabic:	كحولي -[kuħu:l-i:] ("al" is the definite article)	KOD-global: alkol – ik
Bulgarian	алкохол-ен/на/но - alkohol-en/na/no	
Croatian:	alkohol – ni	
English:	alcohol – ic - [ælkə'hɒlɪk]	
Finnish:	alkohol – isti	
German:	alkohol – isch	
Greek:	αλκολικός alkol – ikos	
Italian:	alcol – ico	
Russian:	Алкогольный alkogol'- nyj	
Turkish:	alkol – ik	

-sion, -itet und -ia marking nouns:

The suffix –ia occurs in a majority of the analyzed languages, besides [i] as in German <-ie>, English <-y>, French <-ie>. Choosing -ia as the unified KOD suffix for the respective nouns offers a possibility to clearly distinguish international words from artificially created KOD lexemes. The suffix -sion regularly represents suffixes as German <-tion> [tsion], English <-tion> [ʃən] and their equivalents in other languages. The KOD suffix -itet stands for the following forms in individual languages: German -ität, English -ity, Italian -ita, Hungarian -itás.

-os for names describing persons involved in an activity :

Elements of word formation which display this function in individual languages for instance occur in forms like -or, -er, -ist and -ant.

Bulgarian	фотогра́ф fotograf	KOD-global: fotograf-os
Croatian	fotograf	
English	photograph - er	
Finnish	fotograf - i	
German	Fotograf	
Greek	Φωτογράφος fotograf - os	
Hindi	phoTogrAph- ar	
Hungarian	fotográf- us (old); variant: fotós (informell)	
Italian	fotograf - o	
Russian	Фотограф fotograf	
Turkish	fotoğraf	

III.2. The importance of international words within KOD-global

The notion of international words is often accompanied by the assumption that these words are spontaneously recognized and understood by speakers of other languages[72]. This assumption constitutes a potentially dangerous simplification, however, especially if typologically different languages are considered.

Over and beyond the common interlingual features, which international words display in the domain of phonology or graphology, there are many differences between their representatives in individual languages as well. This also applies to their meaning. Besides interlinguistic correspondences in meaning loaned words

---

[72] This, for instance, is declared to be a property of the linguistic definition for the term "international word" (German "Internationalismus") in the WDG: Wörterbuch der deutschen Gegenwartssprache (1961-1977).

may have assumed a special meaning in a certain language, thus deviating from the meaning associated with that word in most of the other languages. In linguistics such cases are described with the term "faux amis/ false friends".

For this reason it is not intended that international words be integrated into the KOD system under the supposition that their recognition and subsequent comprehension is independent of all context. They are moreover just like all other KOD-lexemes. They constitute units of the KOD-lexicon and are defined there in their relevant meaning.[73] Their main significance lies in their mnemonic utility during the acquisition of vocabulary because they are to be found and easily recognized by the speakers of many different languages.

---

[73] Or meanings, as - in contrast to the general guidelines for KOD-lexemes - an international word may well have more than one well stabilized meaning.

Bibliography to the appendix

Bergmann, Rolf (1995): ‚Europäismus' und ‚Internationalismus'. Zur lexikologischen Terminologie. In: Sprachwissenschaft 20 (1995), p. 239-277

Braun, Peter (1990): Internationalismen – gleiche Wortschätze in europäischen Sprachen. In: Braun, Peter et al. (eds.) (1990): Internationalismen. Studien zur interlingualen Lexikologie und Lexikographie. Tübingen, Max Niemeyer, p. 13-34

Braun, Peter (1999): Internationalismen und Europäismen. Eine lexikologische Analyse. In: Sprachreport 4/1999, p. 20-24

Braun, Peter et al. (eds.) (2003): Internationalismen II, Tübingen: Max Niemeyer

Crystal, David (1997): The Cambridge Encyclopedia of Language. 2nd. edn. Cambridge: Cambridge University Press

Haarmann, Harald (1994): Entstehung und Verbreitung von Alphabetschriften. In: Günther, Hartmut/ Ludwig, Otto (eds.): Schrift und Schriftlichkeit. Writing and Its Use. Ein interdisziplinäres Handbuch internationaler Forschung. 1. Halbband, Berlin/New York: Walter de Gruyter, (=HSK, Vol. 10.1)

Handbook of the International Phonetic Association, Cambridge: University Press 1999

Kolwa, Andrea (2003a): Zur Geschichte der Internationalismus-Forschung. In: Braun, Peter et al. (eds.): Internationalismen II, Tübingen: Max Niemeyer

Kolwa, Andrea (2003b): Probleme der Bestimmung von Internationalismen im Bereich der Politik. In: Braun, Peter et al. (eds.) 2003, p. 51-70

Maddieson, Ian (1984): Patterns of Sounds. Cambridge/London/New York, Cambridge University Press

Martinet A. (1965): La linguistique synchronique. Etudes et recherches. Paris

Özen, Ümit (1999): Internationalismen-Konzeption einer interlexikologischen Theorie. Dargestellt am Beispiel der Ergebnisse einer empirischen Auswertung von türkischen Zeitungstexten. Diss. Siegen, http://www.ub.uni-siegen.de/ epub/diss

Schaeder, Burkhard (1990): Versuch einer theoretischen Grundlegung der Internationalismus-Forschung. In: Braun, Peter et al. (eds.): Internationalismen. Studien zur interlingualen Lexikologie und Lexikographie. Tübingen: Max Niemeyer

Selmy, Elsayed Madbouly (2003): Internationalismen im Arabischen – im Vergleich mit dem Deutschen. Eine empirische Studie. In: EliSe: Essener Linguistische Skripte – in digital form, year 3, volume 2, p. 7-42

Ternes, Elmar (1987): Einführung in die Phonologie. Darmstadt: Wissenschaftliche Buchgesellschaft

Institut für Entwicklung und Forschung

Dr. Vielberth e. K.

Gewerbepark C35
93059 Regensburg
Telefon: (09 41) 4 64 61-0
Telefax: (09 41) 4 64 61-30

Internet: www.eufo-institut.de